Contents

v

Part 3. Contemporary Minorities: Blacks and Chicanos

Vision and Refuge

Essays on the Literature of the Great Plains

Edited by Virginia Faulkner
with Frederick C. Luebke

Published by the University of Nebraska Press
LINCOLN AND LONDON
for the Center for Great Plains Studies
UNIVERSITY OF NEBRASKA–LINCOLN

"Agrarian versus Frontiersman in Midwestern Fiction," by Barbara Meldrum, was first published, in somewhat different form, in *Heritage of Kansas* 11 (Summer 1978): 3–18.

Publishers on the Plains

UNP

Manufactured in the United States of America
The paper in this book meets the guidelines for permanence and durability of the Committee on Production Guidelines for Book Longevity of the Council on Library Resources.

Library of Congress Cataloging in Publication Data
Main entry under title:

Vision and refuge.

Includes bibliographical references and index.
Contents: Black Elk speaks as epic and ritual attempt to reverse history / by Paul A. Olson—Materialism and mysticism in Great Plains literature / by John R. Milton—Agrarian versus frontiersman in Midwestern fiction / by Barbara Meldrum—[etc.]
1. American fiction—History and criticism—Addresses, essays, lectures. 2. Great Plains in literature—Addresses, essays, lectures. I. Faulkner, Virginia, 1913–1980. II. Luebke, Frederick C., 1927–. III. University of Nebraska—Lincoln.
Center for Great Plains Studies.
PS124.V5   810'.9' 978   81–10418
ISBN 0–8032–1960–1   AACR2

6001293302

Preface

SEVEN OF THE EIGHT ESSAYS in this volume were prepared originally for the first and second annual symposia sponsored by the Center for Great Plains Studies, University of Nebraska–Lincoln. Those by Barbara Meldrum, John Milton, Paul Reigstad, and Bernice Slote were presented at the conference on "The Cultural Heritage of the Plains," held in April 1977; the essays by Chester Fontenot, Tomás Rivera, and Dorothy Burton Skårdal were prepared for the symposium on "Ethnicity on the Great Plains," held a year later. The contribution by Paul Olson was written especially for this volume. Selected essays from the 1977 and 1978 symposia exclusive of those treating literary topics have already been published in *The Great Plains: Environment and Culture* (1979), and *Ethnicity on the Great Plains* (1980), both of which I edited, the former with Brian W. Blouet. These volumes brought together work by scholars in history, geography, anthropology, archeology, sociology, and folklore.

The center asked Virginia Faulkner, editor-in-chief of the University of Nebraska Press, to prepare a volume that would bring together the papers on literary topics. *Vision and Refuge* is the result of her efforts. It is the last work to which she devoted her exceptional editorial skills before her death on September 15, 1980. Everyone who knew her, especially her colleagues at the University of Nebraska Press and the authors of scores of books published during her twenty-five years at the press, cherished the quality of her editorial judgment and her keen powers of analysis. For those persons and many others, her death represents a great loss.

The task of completing the editorial work fell to me as an organizer of the symposia and editor of the earlier volumes. Each of the essayists responded readily to my requests for additional revisions and improvements. We are much in their debt for their patience and willing cooperation.

The Center for Great Plains Studies has benefited from the generous support of many persons and agencies in its symposium and publication programs. Among them are the Research Council and the Convocations Committee of the University of Nebraska–Lincoln and the S & H Foundation. Our thanks go to them; the members of the two symposium committees; Paul Olson, the first director of the center; and Max Larsen, Dean of the College of Arts and Sciences.

Frederick C. Luebke
Acting Director
Center for Great Plains Studies

Introduction

THE UNDERLYING PURPOSE of this collection of essays is to encourage systematic study of a large body of writing—fiction and nonfiction, including letters and journals—that, with few exceptions, has only recently begun to receive scholarly attention. The day of the simple answer is long past, but one reason for the late-blooming respectability of western American literature is inherent in American literary history. In the mid-nineteenth century, although natives of the settlements on the banks of the Hudson, the Schuylkill, and the Charles were aware of American expansion westward, the cultural pundits among them assumed that intellectual pursuits could not also migrate to the banks of the Mississippi, the Missouri, and the Platte. In their view the arts in America, particularly the literary art, did not travel.

The idea persisted through subsequent decades. Mari Sandoz's letters of the 1930s and '40s are replete with references to the apathetic attitudes of eastern publishers toward, and their ignorance of, life in whatever period in the stretch of land between the Missouri and the Rockies.[1] In his recent study of western American literature, John R. Milton notes that as recently as 1950 "to ask for full recognition of the western novel (in the academic community) was considered heresy." He observes further that of the fourteen writers to whom he has given most consideration "only two (Cather and Steinbeck) are discussed in the most recent (1974) edition of the standard *Literary History of the United States*," and "two are mentioned only by name (Fergusson and Fisher)." The remaining ten are not even indexed.[2]

The essays of this volume amply demonstrate the importance of Great Plains literature and how it reflects the culture of the people who settled the region. All treat in one way or another how the land was regarded by the people who lived on it: what it represented to them, what they expected from it, and what they brought to it. The essay in Part 1 speaks for one group of the original inhabitants, the Teton Sioux; the contributions to Part 2 express points of view of nineteenth-century newcomers from the eastern United States and Europe; Part 3 offers two articles that record the attitudes of twentieth-century minority groups, blacks and Chicanos.

Paul Olson, in *"Black Elk Speaks* as Epic and Ritual Attempt to Reverse History," shows how the Sioux viewed the plains as a metaphor for a spiritual world. Their perception allowed them to construct a system of symbols or icons that was both culturally and ecologically conservative. Sioux culture permitted individual persons to recreate this iconology with imagination and flexibility. Thus Black Elk used it to state the opposition of his culture to the materialism, faith in progress, and centralized organization that characterized the encroaching European culture. His statement, which is an epic in the traditional sense of the word, came at the nadir of Sioux cultural life. Conveyed to modern readers through John G. Neihardt, it has had considerable influence on both Indians and whites in recent years.

In the opening essay of Part 2, "Materialism and Mysticism in Great Plains Literature," John R. Milton surveys the traditionally materialistic literature of the region from the early travel narratives to the novels of the present day. After the travel narratives, which emphasized information bearing on settlement and commerce, came the farm novels, with their materialistic themes of the struggle to possess and exploit the land. Only as the novel moves westward to the junction of mountain and plain does the mystical element begin to enter in. Milton looks to a new literature of the plains—"a literature of awareness, influenced by the qualities of the land which lead toward mysticism, and supported at the base by an increasing sensitivity to the culture and vision of the American Indian."

Barbara Meldrum, in "Agrarian versus Frontiersman in Midwestern Fiction," questions Frederick Jackson Turner's affirmation of "a unified ideal wherein the best traits of frontiersman and agrarian are combined and are attainable through the cyclical experience which occurs when one is 'reborn' on the frontier and passes through the primitive to the civilized stage of development." Studying the interrelationships of agrarian and frontiersman traits and values in selected novels of three representative writers, Ole Rølvaag, Sophus Keith Winther, and Frederick Manfred, she concludes that while all three writers recognize the existence of "a spirit of rugged individualism marked by courage, fortitude, and love of freedom," nonetheless "frontiersman traits can promote exploitation of the land and domination of other people," while the agrarian ideal "often leads to spiritually unfulfilling materialism." Writing from a frontier perspective, "they all see that physical conquest and movement in space are not necessarily modes of victory."

A novel discussed in the Meldrum essay is examined from another perspective by Paul Reigstad in "Mythic Aspects of *Giants in the Earth.*" The connections with the Faust legend and the ambiguity of Rølvaag's title are explored and elucidated, as well as his "fundamental conception of the prairie as troll-adversary of those who would subjugate it and seize its treasure." Using myth to reinforce his themes, "Rølvaag is saying metaphorically that the frontier experience, apparently happy and successful if only superficially considered, was essentially tragic—costly beyond measure in terms of suffering and human sacrifice."

"Life on the Great Plains in Scandinavian-American Literature" is based on Dorothy Burton Skårdal's extensive study of this fiction, which orginated in ethnic newspapers and magazines around the middle of the nineteenth century. Scrutinizing the novel and stories which bring their characters to the Great Plains, Skårdal finds in them "a superb record of immigrants' judgment, attitudes, feelings about behavioral norms and values within their own group and the host society." Among the themes typical of this literature, the first is the fear of the openness and emptiness of the landscape, which the settlers seek to change by planting trees. Not unexpectedly, the "horrific weather" and natural hazards—rattlesnakes, grasshopper plagues, prairie fires—also figure prominently in the literature of the frontier period. Other common themes include changes in living standards, in farming methods, and in traditional sex roles—" 'People didn't pay much attention to what was women's work or men's work. The main thing was to get done what lay at hand.' " Indians seldom appear in these pioneer novels: they are "simply beyond the European's ken." But novels by first-generation immigrants express bitterness against "the unjust American economic system." Politics (usually conservative), religion (characterized by controversy), alcoholism (the most serious social problem), homesickness (a universal theme), and materialism (the besetting sin) generally play a part in this literature, which illustrates "how the original European heritage was modified by American influences on day-by-day personal experience."

The final essay in Part 2, "Willa Cather and Plains Culture," by Bernice Slote, synthesizes many elements in the four preceding essays. Willa Cather came to Nebraska from Virginia "at one of those turns of history when individual experience is intensified into rebirth" and found in "the unmarked plains . . . the beginning of freedom, growth, fecundity." Her early feeling of homesickness grew into "a sense of passionate identity with the country and the land," which she portrayed in stunning physical detail; and her West was "the West of settlement, of the immigration of many people from many parts of the world—people she saw often as exiles (even as she had once felt the separation from a homeland)." The ancestral myths of home-seeking, the varying cultures of immigrant peoples and the effect of the land upon them, change through growth, and the recession of some values are recorded indelibly in her writing. And though Plains Indians do not figure in her early stories, the novels after her first trip to the Southwest in 1912 "make extensive use of what she observed of Indian qualities and experience." In the body of Willa Cather's work "she fused materials to suggest a world of many lives engaged in the recurring processes of history, the rise and fall of civilizations, of human endeavor."

The essays in Part 3, by Chester J. Fontenot and Tomás Rivera, deal with concepts and problems of sharp concern in the world of the 1980s. In "Oscar Micheaux: Black Novelist and Film Maker," Fontenot details the aims and achievements of the first black writer to portray a black leading character as a pioneer and the first to offer an alternative to black southern life by advocating that black people follow Booker T. Washington's philosophy of economic and moral betterment, not by staying in the South, but by homesteading in the northern Great Plains. As a film maker during the years when "Sambo and Rastus" stereotypes dominated the Hollywood product, Micheaux attempted to deal realistically with the problems of the black middle class, showing them as people whose problems are much like those of white Americans. In his three major novels, *The Conquest, The Homesteader,* and *The Forged Note,* he contrasted the harsh reality of black urban life—"violence, racism, lack of education, unemployment, black-on-black crime—with the utopian environment" of the plains.

Tomás Rivera, himself a novelist, writes in a semi-autobiographical context of "The Great Plains as Refuge in Chicano Literature." As a young man in college, he realized after reading Rølvaag's *Giants in the Earth* that the Chicano workers of the 1940s and '50s were a new breed of giants in the earth and resolved that one day he would tell their story. His essay discusses the concept of refuge in Chicano literature as it has been treated in such firsthand accounts as *The Personal Narration of Elías Garza,* in the *corridos* (ballads) of the late nineteenth and early twentieth century as well as contemporary poetry, and in Rolando Hinojosa-Smith's 1976 novel, *Klail City y sus aldredores* (Klail City and its surroundings), which was awarded the prestigious Premio Casa de las Américas. "It is impossible to imagine Chicano literature without the migrant worker," Rivera concludes, "and it is impossible to imagine the migrant worker without the myriad notions of a refuge in the Great Plains."

NOTES

1. Mari Sandoz Collection, Don L. Love Memorial Library, University of Nebraska, Lincoln, Nebraska.
2. John R. Milton, *The Novel of the American West* (Lincoln: University of Nebraska Press, 1980), pp. vii and xiv.

Part 1

Original Inhabitants
The Teton Sioux

PAUL A. OLSON

Black Elk Speaks as Epic and
Ritual Attempt to Reverse History

CONVENTIONAL CRITICISM of the epic in the Western world has described it as a mixed fiction in which the actions of the gods are to be read as allegory and the actions of the hero as history which teaches by example.[1] The actions of the gods are not seen as "events" that occurred in the sky, outside the historical world; they are, rather, metaphors for forces operating in, or ideas giving meaning to, the history. Achilles, Aeneas, and Odysseus are said to have actually walked the earth and done the deeds recounted when they appear in household or battle contexts; but the Venus who appears as messenger, goddess, temple figure, and guide is described as the planet, the force of passion, or the love that binds the elements. The juxtaposition of men and gods, of human actions and allegorical commentary, is important in that the epic commonly deals with a period of disintegration and reintegration in the history of an area and its peoples. The history reveals what heroic activity is required to stop disintegration and sustain reintegration; the allegory tells what forces the hero must lay hold on.

A comparable distinction appears in Winnebago culture in the difference between *waika* and *worak*. *Waika* stories show what might have been or the sacred meanings of things; they generally end happily. *Worak* stories describe what is or

3

the patterns of things as they are; like most things in this life, they generally end with mixed results. Both anthropologists and the Winnebagoes themselves understand the *waika* stories, especially those concerning sacred beings such as Trickster, Bladder, Hare, and the Twins, as cultural, psychological, or moral allegories.[2]

Modern Siouan storytellers make the same distinction in speaking of the difference between bedtime and sacred stories. Moreover, Lakota masters of the sacred arts are inveterate constructors of figural or allegorical systems. They interpret, apply, and reapply the iconological resources of their culture through ritual, myth, storytelling, symbolic action, and clothing.

This Sioux symbolic tradition is one context in which John G. Neihardt's *Black Elk Speaks* (1932) must be understood. Conceptualizing it as an epic may assist both Western and non-Western readers to clarify the uses to which a culture's symbol system may be put in mediating conflicting values, especially those deemed significant in times of cultural crisis. Neihardt himself was deeply interested in the epic as a literary form. He conceived of his *Cycle of the West* (1941) as a record of the general period of the last three-quarters of the nineteenth century and developed it as an epic. As Neihardt says:

> The period with which the *Cycle* deals was one of discovery, exploration and settlement—a genuine epic period, differing in no essential from the other great epic periods that marked the advance of the Indo-European peoples out of Asia and across Europe. It was a time of intense individualism, a time when society was being cut loose from its roots, a time when an old culture was being overcome by that of a powerful people driven by ancient needs and greeds. For this reason only, the word "epic" has been used in connection with the Cycle. . . . There has been no thought of synthetic *Iliads* and *Odysseys*.[3]

The nineteenth century was a period of great movement for the Lakota people as well as the Euroamericans. Both were threatened by the loss of cultural bonds and by intense individualism. It was a period when an old culture appeared to be dying and a new one was, in Matthew Arnold's phrase, "powerless to be born." It is possible that Neihardt shaped *Black Elk Speaks* as a kind of epic composed from the Lakota perspective to accompany his *Cycle of the West,* which was written, at least in the initial books, from the perspective of the conqueror. A second, more likely, possibility is that Black Elk, as a religious thinker and master of ritual speech, acted at that moment in the life of the Sioux nation when epic as the meaningful combining of allegory and history, was possible and had a function in assisting the culture to survive.[4] Black Elk, like the Homer portrayed in Alfred Lord's *Singer of Tales,* was caught between the recurrent, ritualistic, and formulaic aspects of the old culture, and the record keeping and linear progressions of the new.[5] He chose Neihardt as his scribe just as an oral-formulaic master may have chosen a literate collaborator at some point in the development of the Homeric epic. Neihardt's task was to set down the relationship between the old and the new in Lakota culture. He could communicate Black Elk's vision to others because he was himself a writer for whom the juxtaposition of allegory and historical example which teaches, of religious forces and historic actions, was a possible mode. For him, as for Black Elk, ritual or mystical events do in fact make history outside the events.[6]

For Black Elk, the sacred powers of the directions which he calls "Grandfathers" exist—their powers and cycles are permanent reality, but their capacity to act in the ordinary world which we see has been disrupted by the actions of the white intruders. Black Elk's destiny is not simply that of the common holy man—to keep the cycles alive for a single sick person or for a small group. His burden is to manifest, for his whole exhausted nation, the power of the Grandfathers as they act in the seen world. In representing the sacred harmonies in the dimension of time, he does what every holy man does. But Black Elk's effort to bring the power of the Grandfathers into history and restore history to ritual, to ritual's sacred cycles, takes place on a larger stage than that of any recorded "holy man" in the native tradition of which I have knowledge. His destiny as the bearer of the nation's burden is epic in the traditional sense.

It was fortunate that Black Elk found Neihardt to record his action. Neihardt had schooled himself both in nineteenth-century idealistic philosophy and in the Hindu scriptures. He could understand Black Elk's world, where the world which is seen and felt is but a shadow of another world full of power. No writer whose epistemology is based on naturalistic assumptions could have done the job. Neihardt's fidelity to what Black Elk said is attested by Raymond DeMallie who examined Black Elk's dictations and found only one significant change in the detail of what Black Elk said in Neihardt's literary version. The "reverence and solemnity" that Neihardt introduces from the transcript reflect Black Elk's original spirit. Because Neihardt was interpreting the symbolic structures of a culture not his own, he did not always understand everything Black Elk said through him. However, this does not lessen the significance of the recorder's performance but rather pays tribute to his honesty and fidelity to the material.

The material in *Black Elk Speaks* may be easily divided into the religious-allegorical and the historical. The allegory in the book centers in Black Elk's great vision, his other minor visions, and the five dances which he performs in the early 1880s to act out his great vision. Black Elk glosses this figurative material in part through his explanations of what religious objects such as the pipe or religious actions such as the dances mean. But this explanation usually requires completion through references to glosses of sacred objects offered by Black Elk in other contexts or offered by other holy men to other field workers.

Clearly the great vision requires explanation. In it, Black Elk is carried by the messengers of the thunder into the sky tepee of the Grandfathers, who represent the sacred powers of the four directions and of earth and sky. He is shown the thunder horses of the four directions and, in the east, the rainbow door to the cloud-tepee. Next he is given the symbols of the directions and explanations of each: the cup and the bow for the west, the herb of power for the north, the eagle peace pipe for the east, and the red stick "tree of life" for the

south. He is shown the eagle power of the sky and the re-
generative power of the earth. All of this is relatively clear if
one knows Sioux conventional symbolism, but the remainder
of what happens is much more enigmatic. Black Elk in vision
tries his thunderpower by killing the mysterious blue man
who turns into a turtle and is somehow related to
drouth. The holy man is then instructed to give his people the
sacred emblems of the directions. A great peace reigns until
his people are asked to go through four hills or ascents which
cut across the great circle (or cloud-teepee ring) on which the
four directions are placed. At that point, the holy man appears to witness in vision the stages in some future disintegration of his culture presented in both realistic and symbolic
scenes. And finally, at the end of these ascents, for no reason
apparent to the Western mind, Black Elk finds himself on his
vision stallion again, celebrating the powers of the four directions. The whole restored universe dances, the Grandfathers
celebrate the visionary's triumph, and his spirit, blessing
everything as it goes, returns to his body. This ending is
clearly designed to stand for a hope which will come at the
end of the disasters of the four ascents.

It should be further recalled that each of the five dances
performed later in the book acts out a part of this vision and
its symbolism. These may assist glossing. Visions and dances
then are the central allegory of the book. And these are
intimately connected to the allegory of the powers attributed
to the directions: to the west, where thunder and rain come
from, the power to create and destroy; to the north, with its
seasonal cold, the power of purification; to the east, the power
of wisdom; and to the south, that of growth.

On the other hand, the narrative history in the book
describes the destruction of the self-sufficiency and hope of
the Sioux people between 1863 and 1890 and their efforts to
find enough strength to withstand cultural disintegration.
The story has been told elsewhere, though not with such
tenderness, power of language, sense of dignity in suffering,
and cadenced drumming of disaster's slow coming. Black
Elk's rendering of the history orders the events of the period

by making them the objective reenacting of the four stages on the road to cultural disintegration which he has seen before in his great vision.

The red road ascents or hills, ascents one and two in the vision, cut across the hoop of the world from the south of growth to the north.[7] In ascent one on the red road in the vision, the land is green, the old men and women raise their palms forward to the sky, and the sky is filled with clouds of baby faces (pp. 35–36). In the parallel historical account given later, the first ascent on the red road clearly includes the period up to 1873 and runs through the chapter entitled "High Horse's Counting." In Black Elk's perception, this time is a precontact period. The elders are respected; children are born in a comfortable traditional world and are educated to pursue the old cycles. Courting is controlled by the people,[8] and "two-legs" and "four-legs" appear to collaborate in a harmonious cyclical life.

In ascent two in the vision, the ascent is steeper, the people are changed to elk, bison, and other animals and fowls, and Black Elk floats above them as the power-zenith bird, the spotted eagle (pp. 36–37). The history which is equivalent to this vision appears to begin with the premonitions of a steeper path given to Black Elk and Chips through signs and visions (pp. 77–79); these signs of a white entrance are followed by Custer's incursion into the Black Hills in 1874. The stage runs through the period of the Battle of the Little Bighorn in 1876 and the destruction of the northern buffalo herd in 1883. In the vision, at this time the people are transformed into animals, which symbolizes their reintegration into the cycles of nature, a transformation which also represents a purification. The historical counterpart of this is the five great rituals performed (and in part invented) by Black Elk on the eve of the destruction of the northern herd, rituals in which the celebrants perform the roles of Great Plains creatures or use them sacramentally.

When the ascents move from the south-to-north red road to the east-to-west black road, the sense of disintegration is greatly heightened (pp. 37–38). In the third ascent, the creatures are running around in a disorganized fashion, each following its own rules, the four winds are fighting, and ultimately the nation's hoop is broken. The holy tree is near death and all the birds are gone. The historical unfolding of the third ascent does not begin where Neihardt's chapter title places it, just after the killing of Custer (p. 135). It begins, in Black Elk's narrative, after 1883, when the Sioux become fully aware that the constraints and privations of reservation life are permanent. The majority of the people abandon the circular tepee for the square houses of the white man. Black Elk finds that his people's circumstances clearly reflect his vision. They travel a black road of despair while living in individual square houses scattered in isolated settlements. Their accommodation to white culture means a life in which, as Black Elk expresses it, "everybody [is] for himself and with little rules of his own, as in my vision" (p. 219).[9] The hoop, which symbolizes the nation's unity, is broken; and reservation life shatters the circular authority system and replaces it with the fort and the dole. Inevitably, all other circles of power are weakened or broken.

In the fourth ascent, the people are metamorphosed from animal form back to people again, but starving people; the terror is almost unbearable, the holy tree has disappeared; seen from the fourth ascent on the north side of a camp in the third ascent, a sacred red man appears momentarily—to be metamorphosed to a bison and to the daybreak-star herb, which now stands in the place of the sacred tree. This ascent is never seen in the book since the third ascent continues until 1930, when the book was dictated (p. 37). Earlier, in facing the hunger and despair of his people in the 1880s, Black Elk obviously had held briefly to the notion that the fourth ascent, with its vision of a red-painted sacred man, had been reached by the time of the outbreak of the ghost dance and his own lesser, or "two sticks," vision (pp. 254, 250, 251). It is understandable that Black Elk expected the third ascent's end about the time that the ghost dance broke out in 1890, for each of the earlier ascents had lasted about ten years and he calls the ascents "generations." The manner in which the history which unfolds later glosses the vision is not a matter of certain interpretation even to the visionary.

However, since he finally locates the end of the third ascent in 1930, when the book was told, he must have come to expect that, as the fourth ascent came on, matters would get worse for the Sioux people and the world before any such blessing as the dancing of the universe experienced in the vision would occur in history.

The four ascents as emblems of cultural disintegration represent perverse versions of the constructive power of the quadrants through which they pass. They are destructive because they cut across the cycles of nature in an unnatural order rather than following them.

The ascents, as it were, go from the south of summer to the north of winter to the east of spring and the west of autumn. History makes a society evolve in unnatural sequence. The unnatural character of the ascents does not appear in the first ascent, which is portrayed both in the vision and the comparable historical section as Eden-like. However, the second ascent is less promising. It moves through the north, the direction of sterility and of purification in the vision. In the history which unfolds for the time covered by this quadrant (1873–83), the sterilizing incursions of the white soldiers and the destruction of the fertile buffalo occur. These, for the moment, outweigh in power the purifying rituals which Black Elk performs at the same time and which center in the daybreak-star herb healing ceremony and in the bison dance.

The events which occur at the historical beginning of the suffering of the black road should produce some constructive insight for the people. They are located in the "east" spiritually. The direction is variously called the direction of wisdom (p. 2), of "peace," of the "good red day" (p. 31), the place of the "star of understanding" (p. 180), and the place from which came the messengers who announce the daybreak-star herb part of the great vision (p. 43). East is clearly the place in which visionary insight or intuition is located—the place of new beginnings. Yet the directional power which carries radical strength when a culture is intact also carries the radical possibility for perversion when it is disintegrating. What characterizes the peculiar perversion of the power of the east (the third ascent) is the breaking of the nation's hoop through the appearance of a culture in which each person lives the ethos of "everybody for himself and with little rules of his own" (p. 219), in which each person seemed to "have his own little vision that he followed" (p. 37). The perversion of the power of the east, which occurs as the culture comes apart, represents private mysticism, the appearance of vision so personal and private as to destroy the group sense of itself as a group, a disturbance so tearing that it finds its metaphor in what was for the Teton Dakota the ultimate natural disaster: the warring among the winds.[10] The disintegration of collective into private vision, which destroys the nation's unity, is followed by physical deprivation and the death of the people ("the holy tree") as a people: the death of the sun dance cottonwood tree, of the connection between sky and earth and among the people and the creatures which sustain the people.[11]

The fourth ascent takes the people from the center to the west on the quadrant and embodies the perversion of the power of the west and its thunder: the power to create and to destroy. This ascent in the vision has no counterpart in the history, but it also is dominated by the destructive rather than the creative:

> And when I looked again, I saw that the fourth ascent would be terrible. . . . When the people were getting ready to begin the fourth ascent, the Voice spoke like some one weeping, and it said: "Look there upon your nation." And when I looked down, the people were all changed back to human, and they were thin, their faces were sharp, for they were starving. Their ponies were only hide and bones, and the holy tree was gone. [P. 38][12]

The fourth ascent's destructive aspect is hunger; on the other hand, its creative power is seen only in the ephemeral picture of the sacred man on the north side of the camp who first turned into a bison, then into a sacred herb whose blossoms flashed bright rays. Black Elk thinks for a time that this red man is the messiah whom he sees in his ghost dance vision, but later he regrets that vision "of the two sticks" as he describes it (pp. 251, 254), and in 1930 still places history in the third ascent (p. 37). While the biological path of ascents one and two from generation to sterility is harsh, it is not "terrible," for the collective group can through ritual turn sterility into purification; but the path of ascents three and four, the path of the spirit into the realms of history, is utterly defeating. It destroys the group's resources by turning ritual into private vision; it is attended by physical degradation and ephemeral, meaningless hope. This is the end of history as Black Elk anticipates it for his people; at the same time, his vision ends hopefully with a restoration of everything, and even at the end of the book, the seer seems to have some hope for his people (pp. 279–80).

The disparity between the actual downward movement of the history recounted and the optimism of the great vision and partial hope of its seer even at the end of the book are explicable if one understands the allegory of the great vision and the dances. The great vision and the accompanying rituals of the hoop (the horse dance), the west (the *heyoka* ceremony), the north (the daybreak-star herb healing), the east (the buffalo dance), and the south (the elk dance) are sacred devices. As such they are intended, like the actions of the gods in the ancient epic, to reveal the meaning of history as well as to control it. Black Elk performed these ceremonies between 1880 and 1883, years of crucial suffering for the Sioux because their removal from extended family camps to "farms" along the creek bottoms on the Pine Ridge reservation began in 1879 and continued into the 1880s. The sun dance was forbidden in 1881, and the northern herd wiped out two years later.

The "Offering of the Pipe" section of the book sets forth the basic allegory for all sacred actions celebrating the power of the directions. It is a good place at which to begin the discussion of the intended effect of the rituals:

> These four ribbons hanging here on the stem are the four quarters of the universe. The black one is for the west where the thunder beings live to send us rain; the white one for the north, whence comes the great white cleansing wind; the red one for

the east, whence springs the light and where the morning star
lives to give men wisdom; the yellow for the south, whence
comes the summer and the power to grow. [P. 2]

These coordinates are also equated from east to south to west
to north with the seasons of the year, beginning with spring,
and with the ages of life (babyhood, childhood, adulthood, and
old age).[13] The cycles are recurrent and essentially good.
Hence, for the Black Elk of *The Sacred Pipe*, when the ceremony for the releasing of the soul is performed, the token for
the soul moves through the hole in the tepee, as if being born
out of this world. It goes toward the south into the "childhood"
of the next world on the Milky Way road (cf. p. 195).[14] In most
Lakota ritual (unlike that of, say, the Omaha), the place of
beginning for the ritual is not the spring, the east, or birth
and infancy, but the west of autumn and adulthood. This is in
nature the time when autumn seeds fall and the most creative destruction forces, seeds and frost, are loosed; in human
life, it is the age of responsibility.[15]

Vision controls the culture modifications which Black
Elk makes, particularly those in the dances. The first ritual,
the horse dance, deviates from the conventional pattern of
the dance in a fashion suggested by the great vision.[16]
Whereas the medicine of the horse dance generally is designed to tame outlaw horses, cure sick ones, or make all
kinds perform better, Black Elk makes the dance a cure for
sick people. The changes from the conventional in Black Elk's
performance are made up of details pulled together from the
great vision: (1) the painting of the emblem of the directions
from the great vision on the sacred tepee; (2) the replacement
of the four drummers of the directions by the Six Grandfathers and the creation by the Grandfathers in the sacred
tepee of the red and black roads and the emblems of the four
directions; (3) the presentation of the directional symbols to
the virgins; (4) the singing of songs directed to the powers of
the quarters; and (5) the substitution by Black Elk of the
eagle feather emphasizing prophetic sky power for the buffalo horns on the shaman's mask. Completely conventional,
on the other hand, are the painting of the horses and riders,
the organizing of participants in the ceremony into direc-

tional groups, the circling of the sacred hoop, the costumes, and the charging of the sacred tepee. Black Elk's changes, however, make the ritual over from a horse-control ritual to one which does what the recently repressed sun dance did while it was allowed. It celebrates the unbroken hoop of the nation prior to its breaking in history, unites the male and female powers of the four directions, and gives access to the prophetic voice of the Six Grandfathers, which are aspects of the power that moves the world.

The ritual also acts to remind Black Elk and the reader of the uses of ritual based on the notion that the material world is to greater or lesser degrees a shadow of the spiritual:

> Then the Grandfathers behind me sang another sacred song from my vision, the one that goes like this:
>   "At the center of the earth, behold a four-legged.
>   They have said this to me!"
> And as they sang, a strange thing happened. My bay pricked up his ears and raised his tail and pawed the earth, neighing long and loud to where the sun goes down. And the four black horses raised their voices, neighing long and loud, and the whites and the sorrels and the buckskins did the same; and all the other horses in the village neighed, and even those out grazing in the valley and on the hill slopes raised their heads and neighed together. Then suddenly, as I sat there looking at the cloud, I saw my vision yonder once again—the tepee built of cloud and sewed with lightning, the flaming rainbow door, and underneath, the Six Grandfathers sitting, and all the horses thronging in their quarters; and also there was I myself upon my bay before the tepee. I looked about me and could see that what we then were doing was like a shadow cast upon the earth from yonder vision in the heavens, so bright it was and clear. I knew the real was yonder and the darkened dream of it was here.
> And as I looked, the Six Grandfathers yonder in the cloud and all the riders of the horses, and even I myself upon the bay up there, all held their hands palms outward toward me. [Pp. 172–73]

The function of this ritual for Black Elk is both to permit a glimpsing of the pattern and to make history follow it. The ceremony ends with dancing, with a healing which indicates that it is efficacious, and with a final plunge to the tepee at the center which stands for the Sacred Tree of the collective, a tepee in which the special horses of the spirit world have also been dancing.

The succeeding dances refer more specifically to the history of the period and the history which is to come after 1883. The first, the west or *heyoka* ceremony, is preceded by Black Elk's vision in which the Sioux people act the role of butterflies, the white hordes act the role of dogs, and the daybreak-star herb promises to heal all. Because of the vision, the ceremony which follows can use the dog sacramentally to stand for white culture, so that the relief promised by the dance is relief from that culture, not from drouth. Black Elk and his colleagues capture the heart and head of the dog while acting the role of the thunders, as the other heyokas crazy-act the roles of drought-relieving rain and growth, and the people gain a sense of strength and relief from despair.[17] Even as plants and rivers need the destructive power of the heyoka man's thunders to renew the natural order, so the people need to consume the destructive power of the dog, the white man of the vision, to renew their hope and gain relief from bleakness.

The ceremony of the north is the daybreak-star herb healing. In the dog vision, the daybreak-star herb appears juxtaposed against the sickness of the people, apparently to call attention to its northern, or healing, aspect. Normally, a purification rite for the Sioux people would be the sweatlodge ceremony,[18] but Black Elk, on the basis of his dog-butterfly vision, substitutes the daybreak herb healing for "what one might expect to find." In the great vision, the daybreak-star plant appears as a replacement both for the buffalo and the "savior," the red holy man of the vision. The Sioux assign tremendous power to vision as a tool in shaping culture and in understanding and using nature. Thus, in his manner of selecting a medicinal herb on the basis of a vision, Black Elk does nothing unusual. For example, the Brule herbal medicine person, Richard Fool Bull, indicated that his father, the holy man Fool Bull, received an understanding of his

unique medicines—water, calamus, and compass plant—
from visions.[19]

A knowledgeable observer of Sioux herbal lore has told
me that she believes Black Elk's daybreak herb was perhaps
comfrey, a plant which does in fact have the thick root which
Black Elk assigns to it and which may have the yellow, red,
blue, and white flowers which appear so distinctly as to make
it a medicine-wheel plant.[20] That the plant has a location in
vision and a parallel one in the natural world is no more
surprising than that this world is the shadow of another. If
the decongestant powers of comfrey make the healing
through drawing the northern purifying wind through the
sick boy seem to have a natural explanation to us, from a
Sioux perspective the healing is no more or less su-
pernatural—no more or less a matter of laying hold on the
power offered by vision—than would be the healing through
water practiced by Fool Bull. But the purification needed
here is not the sweat bath, or spiritual cleansing, but plain
physical healing. In the journey west through the last two
ascents which cut across the hoop, private vision leads to
social despair and physical sickness; in the ritual journey
around the hoop, the communal vision of the horse dance for
the whole hoop leads to two actions contrary to that of the last
two ascents: a ceremony which promotes social hope (the
heyoka ceremony) and one which creates physical healing
(the daybreak-ceremony healing).

The third ceremony in the progress around the hoop, the
bison ceremony, acts out the great vision's picture of the
power of the east. It tells how "a red man turned into a bison
and rolled" (cf. pp. 28 and 209). Black Elk associates the
ceremony with finding the good red road again, an association which would appear to project the power of the ceremony
far into the future since the people are historically not yet
even on the black road in 1883. Historically, they are just
about to leave the red road, to endure the black. Yet, the red
road is celebrated in the ritual. Since the east is the direction
of power, vision, and of community mystical understanding
when rightly appropriated and of private vision when

wrongly, one would expect the ceremony of this direction to be a community celebration of vision and illumination such as the sun dance was. But Black Elk performs only a variant of the bison fertility-hunt ceremony. On the surface, it seems to say in addition only that the people and the bison depend on each other. The rite is a curious one to be performing and to regard as a success at the very time when the last of the northern herd was being extinguished.[21] But the statement of the ritual is deeper, as Black Elk warns: at the center of the sacred place Black Elk adds several symbols, as he has in earlier rites—the buffalo-wallow symbol for earth and for the bison-power of earth. Above the circle and wallow he sets the tepee, symbol of sky power. Across this circle, he adds the symbol of the red road followed by tracks symbolic of the power and endurance of the animal. When the symbols of the people walk the bison-red-road, they are portrayed as moving through the wind of purification toward what I would take to be creation or recreation—the water of life symbol wrenched from the west to undo the disintegrative power of the black road, on which the people are about to walk historically. And Black Elk as holy man fuses the bison power of the earth, represented in his being painted red, with the eagle power of the sky, represented by the eagle feather of his right horn; he fuses both powers with that of the new sky-earth symbol represented by the daybreak-star herb on his buffalo's western horn.[22]

The chant of the Buffalo rite seems to portray the people acquiring the sacred medicine power of the defunct bison, uniting the sky power of the eagle with the earth power of the bison through the action of the recreative daybreak-star herb. This herb, as its symbolism and action suggest, is simultaneously healing and vision, and it both flashes in the sky and grows from the earth (p. 190, pp. 201–2):

> Revealing this, they walk.
> A sacred herb—revealing it, they walk.
> Revealing this, they walk.
> The sacred life of bison—revealing it, they walk.
> Revealing this, they walk.

A sacred eagle feather—revealing it, they walk.
Revealing them, they walk.
The eagle and the bison—like relatives they walk.

[P. 211]

Black Elk through the ceremony summarizes the strength of the collective vision of the hoop-defined-east as opposed to the "each one his own little vision" power of the black-road-defined-east in his most explicit comment on the meaning of a ceremony: "It is from understanding [i. e., mystical understanding] that power comes; and the power in the ceremony was in understanding what it meant; *for nothing can live well except in a manner that is suited to the way the sacred Power of the World lives and moves*" (p. 212; italics added). Having almost lost the buffalo and being about to lose for a time the sacred vision of the eagle (which I take to stand for the sun dance religion ceremony), Black Elk enacts for his people a vision of harmonious being within the circle of life depending not on the buffalo and the eagle, but on the sacred power behind the bison and the eagle and the world itself ("where you must move in measure like a dancer"). The ritual seems to say that the displacement of the traditional vehicles of the sacred power does not displace the power of the circle-religion, though it may require new symbols or a more direct reliance on the movement of the "Power of the World." Not accidentally, the ceremony of collective vision leads to collective healing (pp. 211–12).

The elk ceremony is the final ceremony to pull the hoop together. As the ceremony of the south, it combines the male and female forces in a sacred unification like that of Okaga, the power of the south, and Wohpe, the white buffalo calf woman, who is the power of the center in the Sioux story of the original creation. The ceremonial march of *Black Elk Speaks* around the directions from west to north to east to south ending in the center, is recollective of the Sioux sacred creation story of the first laying out of the boundaries of the universe and setting of the directions, which also takes place in the same order.[23] Black Elk, faced with the collapse of his culture, had to lay out the paradigm again. Everything in the ceremony stresses the interdependency of the male and the female, of sky and earth, in the circling of the living seasons. The women have on them colors suggestive of male sky power and have sky luminaries painted on their faces; the males are painted with the colors of the female earth power and wear masks suggestive of the female, "for behind the woman's power of life is hidden the power of man." In developing the ceremony from its traditional form, Black Elk appears to elaborate the symbolism of the four directions and the complementarity of the male / female symbolism, placing sky symbols on the four virgins though they wear earth scarlet colors (pp. 212–13). He places hoop symbols and flowering stick symbols painted earth red on the men though their yellow painting emphasizes "light" or sky colors.

Black Elk also elaborates the return to the tepee of the old elk dance. When the flowering tree is placed at the south of the sacred areas, as in the "Ceremony for the Releasing of the Soul," it stands for the individual; when it is moved to the center it stands for the nation.[24] Thus, Black Elk's movement of the flowering-stick symbols from the south to the center at the end of the ceremony symbolizes the rebirth of the nation as a nation; the placing of the "flowering tree" at the center is a ritualistic putting back of the sun-dance tree or its spiritual equivalent. The "centering" action is a particularly poignant ritualistic action in 1883 in view of the suppression of the sun dance in 1881. The ritual celebrates the completion of the four directions, the circling of men around woman, of sky around earth, and finally moves from the south, the place of fruition and growth, to the center, where the collective is always located.

The south of the red road in the ascent vision, representing a stable state culture, pictures only children and elders blessing the world; the south of the elk dance, representing a recreative process in the life of a nation tormented by starvation, emphasizes sexuality and generation. It should be observed that the symbolism both of the great vision and of the rituals is traditional in almost every detail.[25] Vision-seeing is fundamentally a culture-bound art. We dream and see visions in the emblems which make up our education. But in Black Elk's case the spiritual sight is more impersonal than usual because his applications of traditional emblems to historic circumstances are almost entirely directed toward the crisis in the nation's life, rather than to the pain of anyone's private circumstances. It is as if the great dream and the rituals which set it out were an answer to the impending emergence of a culture in which each person followed his own little vision and acted "everybody for himself and with little rules of his own." The function of the five rituals is superficially to do what a thunder being, or *heyoka*, is required to do: to act out the great thunder's vision so that its power will be available to the dreamer and his people.[26]

In putting on the ceremonies, Black Elk does something altogether usual in using traditional figurative resources and simultaneously something unique in arranging the ceremonies to complete the hoop of the world step by step, so as to make each step apply to an aspect of the way in which history has destroyed, or is about to destroy, the great circling. The roads of cultural disintegration of the ascents proceed from generation (south) to sterility or purification (north) to private vision (east) and ultimately to complete terror and deprivation (west). The road of integration of the rituals moves from the recreation of hope (west) to the recovery of health (north), collective vision (east), and procreative power (south). The rituals are the creative side of the destructive power of the ascents and are creative because they are placed in nature's order. The ritual section ends in the reconstruction of the people—the holy tree at the center of the hoop. These reconstitutive stages are as certain in their order as autumn, winter, spring, and summer, or as the ages in the life of a man or a people.

The power of the first two rituals of the west and north is carried into history. Using the west's ritual perception, Black Elk ventures into the white world and sees its power and limitations in the trip with Buffalo Bill to Europe. He draws on the power of the north when he assumes the role of the goose at Wounded Knee and flies the vision flight to rally his people. It may be that he performs the action of the third stage, the restoration of collective vision, through giving Neihardt (or "Flaming Rainbow" from his vision) his great

vision.[27] He also gave Joseph Epes Brown the rituals of his
people so that the iconology and values, the ritual statement,
of the great vision of the people would be maintained. But the
undoing of the evils of the fourth ascent, the death of the holy
tree, in the action of the elk ritual, which iconologically
replaces the holy tree, is not completed. That is the import of
Black Elk's summary statement and his final prayer:

> You see me now a pitiful old man who has done nothing, for the
> nation's hoop is broken and scattered. There is no center any
> longer, and the sacred tree is dead. [P. 276]

> Here, old, I stand, and the tree is withered, Grandfather, my
> Grandfather! [P. 279]

Then the old man concedes that the tree may not be dead:

> Again, and maybe the last time on this earth, I recall the great
> vision you sent me. It may be that some little root of the sacred
> tree still lives. Nourish it then, that it may leaf and bloom and
> fill with singing birds. [P. 279–80]

The old man, Lear-like in his near blindness and seeming
impotence, has done nothing and yet he has done everything,
for he has kept alive a vision and moved the powers of three of
its directions into history. That of the fourth direction can be
left to nature's reproductive power. To say that one has done
nothing is to be ultimately vulnerable, but it is also to be,
paradoxically, completely the vehicle of the "Power that
Moves the World."

Conventionally, the Western epic ends with the triumph
of the culture which possesses both wisdom and fortitude over
the culture which possesses simply violence.[28] The promise of
the epic is the promise of an empire which will be above the
native peoples and rule them well, teaching them to subdue
the beast in themselves and that nature which is around
them. It is hard to reckon the influence which two thousand
years of schoolboy reading of Virgil may have had on the
notions of empire and of manifest providential destiny which
our culture has developed.[29] Neihardt's own *Cycle of the West*
is different from the traditional Western epic in that it represents the conquering civilization as destroyed—hollowed

out—by its own materialism and individualism. The normative statement for the *Cycle* epic is put in the mouth of Sitting Bull, a statement which Neihardt loved to recite in his old age:

> Have I not seen the only mother, Earth,
> Full-breasted with the mercy of her Springs,
> Rejoicing in her multitude of wings
> And clinging roots and legs that leaped and ran?
> And whether winged or rooted, beast or man,
> We all of us were little ones at nurse.
> And I have seen her stricken with a curse
> Of fools, who build their lodges up so high
> They lose their mother, and the father sky
> Is hidden in the darkness that they build;
> And with their trader's babble they have killed
> The ancient voices that could make them wise.
> Their mightiest in trickery and lies
> Are chiefs among them.[30]

The action of *Black Elk Speaks* is an effort, through Neihardt as "Flaming Rainbow," to bring into history the ritualistic forces that will stop history itself as the white man has shaped it and restore to the Sioux people the old ritualistic and cyclical year which gave them their strength. Black Elk's vision is not Quixotic. It was not a Sioux holy man but an adviser to an international group of futurists, computer experts, and economists who observed that a primary defect of the industrial way of life is that it cannot be sustained, and that if we do not choose to change, "the natural system by its internal processes will choose for us."[31] And it was not romanticism but a tough-minded analysis of mankind's future options that led the British Society for the Survival of Mankind to propose that we examine seriously something like the old Sioux way of relating to the climax ecosystem of the Plains and to the buffalo as a model for the construction of any future society's relation to nature.[32] The same analysis suggests that industrial man has lost his hoop by losing track of his roots, his relation to the natural process, and his former sense of organized, small-group community.

One cannot know whether such a society can be created

apart from the spiritual resources which sustained Sioux civilization. Even from the perspective of Western culture, it may have been something more than superstition which led Black Elk to perform his dream in the world and hope that the power of rituals would force history back into the cyclical and constantly regenerating mold of the seasons. Modern man may also have to learn that "nothing can live well except in a manner that is suited to the way the sacred Power of the World lives and moves."

NOTES

I am indebted to Elaine Jahner, Frederick Luebke, Leslie Whipp, Joseph Young, and Kay Young for assistance throughout this essay.

1. Paul A. Olson, "Of Noon Scholars and Old Schools," *PMLA* 31 (1966): 20; the notion of the mixed fiction is treated in commentaries on the epic by Servius, Bernardus Silvestris, Boccaccio, Landino, Harrington, Sidney, Pope, and others.

2. Paul Radin, *The Road of Life and Death* (New York: Pantheon, 1945), p. 54.

3. John G. Neihardt, *A Cycle of the West* (New York: Macmillan, 1949), pp. v–vi. The one-volume paperback edition of this work, published by the University of Nebraska Press, is out of print. At the author's request it was reissued in two volumes: *The Mountain Men* and *The Twilight of the Sioux* (Lincoln: University of Nebraska Press, Bison Books, 1971). Volume 1 includes *The Song of Three Friends*, *The Song of Hugh Glass*, and *The Song of Jed Smith*. Volume 2 includes *The Song of the Indian Wars* and *The Song of the Messiah*. Both volumes carry the Introduction cited in this essay.

4. In later versions, the book is said to be "told through John G. Neihardt (Flaming Rainbow)." John G. Neihardt, *Black Elk Speaks* (1932; reprint ed., Lincoln: University of Nebraska Press, 1979), title page. The text of the 1961 University of Nebraska Press Bison Book edition, now out of print, has identical pagination. All quotations and references are to the Nebraska editions.

5. Albert Lord, *The Singer of Tales* (Cambridge: Harvard University Press, 1964), pp. 124–57.

6. John G. Neihardt, *All Is But a Beginning* (New York: Harcourt Brace Jovanovich, 1972), pp. 48–51; cf. Neihardt, *Poetic Values: Their Reality and Our Need of Them* (New York: Macmillan, 1925), *passim*, esp. pp. 71–73, and p. 98.

7. In *Black Elk Speaks*, as the people begin the first ascent on the red road, the south is a voice behind them (p. 36); the red road ascent also heads north in the bison dance (p. 210). The same directional thrust for the red and black roads is posited by Neihardt in *When the Tree Flowered* (1951; reprint ed., Lincoln: University of Nebraska Press, Bison Books, 1970), p. 47.

The red road and the black road are described as follows by Joseph Epes Brown in *The Sacred Pipe* (Baltimore: Penguin Books, 1973), p. 7: "The 'red road' is that which runs north and south and is the good or straight way, for to the Sioux the north is purity and the south is the source of life. This 'red road' is thus similar to the Christian 'straight and narrow way'; it is the vertical of the cross, or the *ec-circata el-mustaquium* of the Islamic tradition. On the other hand, there is the 'blue' or 'black road' of the Sioux, which runs east and west and which is the path of error and destruction. He who travels on this path is, Black Elk has said, 'One who is distracted, who is ruled by his senses, and who lives for himself rather than his people.' "

8. For an account of the disastrous effects on the Teton Sioux of the breakup of their traditional courting patterns, see Gordon Macgregor, *Warriors without Weapons* (Chicago: University of Chicago Press, 1946), pp. 111–20. The chapter concerning High Horse's courting (pp. 67–76), with its innocent picture of the older generation's control of his clownish courting, is crucial to the first-ascent Edenic picture and also to the understanding of the power that the later elk dance is to restore.

9. For useful discussions of anomie that provide social-science equivalents of Black Elk's treatment of the "disease," see Jan Van Den Berg, *The Changing Nature of Man* (New York: Norton, 1961), and Marshall Clainaird, *Anomie and Deviant Behavior* (New York: Free Press, 1964). Part of the Black Road begins around 1878 (p. 157).

10. The notion of the "warring among the winds" may reflect the contest of Eya, Yata, Yanpa, and Okaga; for published accounts, see Royal B. Hassrick, *The Sioux* (Norman: University of Oklahoma Press, 1967), pp. 208–12; J. R. Walker, "The Sun Dance and Other Ceremonies of the Oglala Division of the Teton Dakota," *Anthropological Papers of the American Museum of Natural History* 16, no. 2 (1917): 169–81.

11. For the holy tree as temporarily and literally the sun-dance cottonwood tree, see Brown, "The Sun Dance," in *The Sacred Pipe*, p. 69. Black Elk's picture of the death of the holy tree may be associated with the actual historical forbidding of the sun dance to the Teton Dakota by the government in 1881.

12. Wallace Black Elk, who is regarded by some as an effective *Wichasha Wakan*, speaks of the Teton people as now being in the

fourth ascent and sees the difficulties for the nation growing worse. Speech at the University of Nebraska–Lincoln, 1974.

13. Cf. *Black Elk Speaks*, pp. 203–4; cf. Walker, "The Sun Dance," pp. 159–60; Black Elk also calls the south the quadrant "whence comes the summer" (p. 2).

14. Brown, *The Sacred Pipe*, p. 29. The hair-lock bundle, which stands for the soul, is passed from the south around the tepee to the north and out the east door (p. 22), and out toward the Milky Way "Spirit Path" (p. 29).

15. For Omaha equivalents of Sioux iconology (as described in Walker, Brown, and Neihardt), see Lawrence J. Evers, "Native American Oral Literature in the College English Classroom," *College English* 36 (1975): 649–62; and Paul A. Olson, *The Book of the Omaha* (Lincoln: Nebraska Curriculum Development Center, 1980).

16. Clark Wissler, "Societies and Ceremonial Associations of the Oglala Division of the Teton Sioux," *Anthropological Papers of the American Museum of Natural History* 11, no. 1 (1912): 1–101; cf. the account in Amos Bad Heart Bull, *A Pictographic History of the Oglala Sioux*, text by Helen Blish (Lincoln: University of Nebraska Press, 1967), pp. 198–99, and 279, and the account by Edward Fasthorse in the possession of Elaine Jahner, Lincoln, Nebraska.

17. Paradoxically, Black Elk's "great vision" is not the product of his vision quest; his "dogs and butterflies" vision is. The *heyoka* ceremony thus integrates a tribute to the Grandfather of the west, seen in the great vision, with a performing of Black Elk's second "thunder vision," the vision-quest vision of dogs and butterflies. For the accounts of the *heyoka* ceremony, see Wissler, "Societies and Ceremonial Associations," pp. 82–88; John Fire and Richard Erdoes, *Lame Deer: Seeker of Visions* (New York: Simon and Schuster, 1972), pp. 242–46. For the meaning of the sacramentalizing of an object, see Claude Lévi-Strauss, *The Savage Mind* (Chicago: University of Chicago Press, 1968), pp. 233–35.

18. Cf. Brown, *The Sacred Pipe*, pp. 31–43.

19. I have these observations from Richard Fool Bull.

20. I initially received this suggestion from Kay Young; subsequently, Larry Webb established that comfrey conformed in all its details to the description of the daybreak-star medicine-wheel herbs. For the standard botanical description of comfrey, see Nathaniel L. Britton et al., *An Illustrated Flora of the Northern United States* (New York: Botanical Gardens, 1943), p. 92. L. C. Bailey, *Manual of Cultivated Plants* (New York: Macmillan, 1969), p. 386, observes that *Symphytum officinale*, or comfrey, has white, yellowish, and purple or rose flowers. Some herbals note that the *Symphytum* may bear these various colored flowers on one plant or stem.

21. The bison ceremony was performed in the summer of 1882; Black Elk places the slaughter of the last of the northern herd in the fall of 1883. The last great buffalo hunt was undertaken in 1882.

22. The buffalo-dreamer dance went as follows: "When they had a dance, a shaman would appear in the head and skin of a buffalo. As he ran about the camp, a nude young man stalked him, while the cult followed singing. At the proper time, the hunter discharged an arrow deeply into a spot marked on the buffalo skin. The shaman would then stagger, vomit blood and spit-up an arrow point. The wolf cult would then pursue him. Later another shaman would use medicine, pull the arrow out and at once the wound was healed" (Wissler, "Societies and Ceremonial Associations," pp. 91–92). Members would bellow like buffaloes and stamp a foot on the ground, leaving a buffalo track. Hassrick notes that "the dreamer of the buffalo wearing a buffalo hide with head and horns attached, often painted a circle on his back which served as a target" and a strong dreamer could repel the missile (*The Sioux*, p. 32). The buffalo wallow which Black Elk incorporates into the iconology of his buffalo dance appears to have been taken over from the buffalo sing menstrual rites (cf. *The Sioux*, pp. 260–61; *The Sacred Pipe*, p. 122).

23. The story of Okaga and Wohpe is in the epic of the setting down of the four directions, which is recorded in materials gathered by the physician and anthropologist James R. Walker. Materials in the Walker Collection are being published in several volumes, the first of which has been published as *Lakota Belief and Ritual*, ed. Raymond DeMallie and Elaine Jahner (Lincoln: University of Nebraska Press, 1980).

24. Cf. note 14 above.

25. For example, in the great vision the iconology of the horses (from the horse dance), of the tepee as the sky, of the Six Grandfathers as the four directions and earth and sky, of the living tree, of eagle and buffalo, of the hoop, and of the west, north, and south are completely conventional.

26. Cf. Fire and Erdoes, *Lame Deer: Seeker of Visions*, pp. 241–42. "What I mean is that a man who has dreamed about thunderbirds . . . he has to act out his dream in public" (p. 241). Fire speaks as if the *heyoka* has to act out his dream in public the very day of the dream; however, no temporal injunctions are attached to Calico's acting out of his dream save the notion that prior to acting out the dream the dreamer is in danger of being killed by lightning (Wissler, "Societies and Ceremonial Associations," pp. 1–101). Calico says, "After this I realized that I must formally tell in the ceremony exactly what I experienced." Black Elk allows eleven years to go by between the great vision (1872) and the elk ceremony, which completes his performing of all segments of the dream (1883).

27. I once heard Neihardt say that Black Elk had not failed in that his great vision was still efficacious. He then explained the

relationship between the flaming rainbow which appears in the great vision and his own Indian name, as I have explained it here. The logic of naming in Sioux culture would suggest the same interpretation. Black Elk did fail to use his anti-white medicine (cf. Missouri MSS).

28. Cf. Robert E. Kaske, *"Sapientia et Fortitudo* as Controlling Theme in *Beowulf," Studies in Philology* 55 (July 1958): 423–57.

29. Cf. J. W. Mackail, *Virgil, and His Meaning to the World of Today* (New York: Longmans, 1930), p. 111; Alexander G. McKay, *Virgil's Italy* (Greenwich: New York Graphic Society, 1970), pp. 50–52; Mario A. DiCesare, *The Altar and the City: A Reading of Virgil's Aeneid* (New York: Columbia University Press, 1974), pp. 94–123.

30. Neihardt, *The Song of the Messiah,* p. 78. See note 3, above; the pagination is the same in the Macmillan and the Bison Book editions.

31. *Collected Papers of J. W. Forrester,* ed. Jay W. Forrester (Cambridge, Massachusetts: Wright-Allen, 1973), p. 221.

32. Edward Goldsmith et al., *Blueprint for Survival* (Boston: Houghton Mifflin, 1972), pp. 103–7.

Part 2

Nineteenth-Century Immigrants The Euro-American Experience

JOHN R. MILTON

Materialism and Mysticism in Great Plains Literature

TRADITIONALLY, the European-American literature of the Great Plains and of the entire West has been materialistic in attitude and theme. This comes as no surprise, since the exploration and settlement of the West were prompted chiefly by materialistic values. We think of the frontier movement as a part of the American dream, but we are often misled by the associations between dreamer and visionary. Although the dream had religious sanctions (Manifest Destiny was more than political), it was grounded in a concept of Eden that was less biblical than it was a gospel of greed. Americans went west for adventure, free land, beaver pelts, buffalo robes, gold, silver, and copper. Even those who went with the blessing of a church did so in order to convert the "heathen" Indians to a religion becoming increasingly materialistic in its own right, and when their efforts failed, they joined others in calling for the extinction of the savage.

Materialism is more than the desire for possessions, even though its most obvious nineteenth-century manifestation lay in the acquisition of territory and therefore encompassed all of American expansion. It is also a love of action, of expediency, of visible achievement, and of progress—all

characteristics of the American frontier. It is essentially naturalistic in its competitiveness, but it can also be romantic in
its pursuit of an ideal that can presumably be purchased, or at
least achieved through the workings of wealth. It embodies
secularism and plurality. The American Indian, more mystical than the white man in his relationship to the natural
world and to some kind of divine being, found it difficult to
understand the materialism of the white man's churches.
There must have been also a deep wonder about the number
of religious organizations, all professing to believe in the
same God and yet competing for converts.

The first written accounts by Englishmen or Americans
of the plains country ignore those elements of Indian religion
that later become one of the sources of mysticism in plains
literature. In 1766 Jonathan Carver, then in Minnesota,
dismissed Indian religious principles as "rude and unin-
structed." His interest was mainly in the abundance of rice,
fruit trees, meadows of hops, nuts and roots, and sugar-
producing maple trees, all of which were "sufficient for any
number of inhabitants." His map projects the plains from
Minnesota to the South Sea, and he envisioned an empire (the
center of which he placed at present-day St. Paul) that would
literally feed the world.[1] His commercial view of the West
was later shared by Lewis and Clark to the extent that their
expedition sought a waterway to the Pacific Ocean, an opening to trade with the oriental countries. Along the way, as
their journals indicate, they were intent upon recording the
details of the land newly acquired by the United States. Since
the journals were written in response to orders from Presi-
dent Thomas Jefferson, it may be unfair to say that they
constitute a catalogue of materialistic concerns; yet, in their
own way they survive as a kind of literature, human, often
vivid, sometimes exciting, frequently romantic as the men
gaze in awe at the landscape. Nevertheless, on only one
occasion did Lewis feel that he had experienced something
"mysterious and unaccountable," when on 14 June 1805 a
monstrous bear that was pursuing him suddenly stopped and
ran away. In expanding this episode in *Tale of Valor*, a historical novel based upon the Lewis and Clark expedition, Vardis

Fisher mildly charges several pages with at least suggestions of nature mysticism, describing mysteries which rival those of the whale in *Moby Dick*.[2] The animals— creatures—cannot be fully understood even though many scientific facts are available.

For most of the travelers on the plains in the early nineteenth century the land was viewed merely in terms of possible commerce and settlement. Some of the reports were negative, some were overly enthusiastic, and a few were objective. For Stephen Long, crossing the plains in 1820, the place was a desert—the Great American Desert—to be dismissed from all thoughts of settlement.[3] Josiah Gregg's four round trips across the plains to Santa Fe between 1831 and 1840 taught him a great deal about the land and about commerce, but he saw little of the spirit.[4] His *Commerce of the Prairies* has been called a moral and natural history, and rightly so, but its extreme objectivity is broken only a few times by moral or social indignation, never by recognition of signs of a spirit world existing on the fringes of his commercial enterprises. In 1839, Joseph Nicollet, traveling through the land of the Dakotas, saw and mentioned a locality that was supposed to be sacred to the Indians, but he expressed no interest in it. What held his attention was the richness of the river valleys and the monotony of the "interminable plains," an extreme tedium which affected his men until they were partially relieved by "bi-carbonate of soda."[5] Farther south, in 1832, Washington Irving described the landscape through allusions to Europe, seeing the Indians largely as stately, sculpted figures. In a grand manner he proposed that America's youth should be sent on a tour of the prairies to acquire "that manliness, simplicity, and self-dependence most in unison with our political institutions."[6] Lewis Garrard's *Wah-to-yah and the Taos Trail* is a great adventure, full of the speech of the mountain men and of sensitively recorded scenes combining action and description in the manner of the novelist, but the emphasis is on people and their customs and the tone is often matter-of-fact: "The object of the expedition, in which we were about to engage, was to travel as far as we could toward Taos; kill and scalp every

Mexican to be found, and collect all the animals belonging to the Company and the United States."[7] When he finally speaks of the harmony of nature, an implication of something in the land that is more than its simple physical presence, it is in a sentence which must be judged suspect for its tone: "We were under the influence of the harmony of nature, tobacco, and Taos whiskey."[8] It is difficult, because of the association with smoking and drinking, to give to the word "harmony" the importance that it might deserve. Yet it is also difficult to dismiss altogether the possibility that Garrard, like many other observers of the western landscape, might have felt something toward nature that he was unable to explain more fully. The seeds of intuitive thought and mystical response lie just below the surface of the more easily recognizable materialistic attitude of many nineteenth-century western travelers.

As Garrard was beginning his journey in 1846, Francis Parkman was well on his way in the big swing around the plains, out on the Oregon Trail and back on the Santa Fe Trail. His youthfulness may have kept him from recognizing the important events taking place in the West that year, but it may also have enabled him to come close to one or two insights into the essences of the plains. A few days from the Platte, on the way out, in the course of a melodramatically romantic evening, he suddenly realized that he "and the beasts were all that had consciousness for many a league around." It is likely that he did not identify completely with the horses; it is possible that his reading of Emerson influenced him momentarily. In either case, he seemed to catch a fleeting glimpse of the oneness of nature. A few days later, on seeing the Platte for the first time, he describes the view as "right welcome; strange, too, and striking to the imagination, and yet it had not one picturesque or beautiful feature; nor had it any of the features of grandeur, other than its vast extent, its solitude, and its wildness." His language, from another country, did not allow him to discover the uniqueness of the plains. Yet he knew that something was wrong.[9] What he did not seem to know was that the western landscape demanded a new kind of perception and a new language to take into account the peculiar beauty of the plains and mountains.

The literature of the Great Plains thus begins with the travel narrative of the first half of the nineteenth century. It is understandable that its emphasis should be on the reporting of facts which would have some bearing upon the feasibility of settlement, the possibility of commerce, and the outward feelings of the Indians who might pose an obstacle to expansion of the union of states. It is a practical literature, in spite of many fine passages that can be approached in literary terms. Its aims were materialistic, even to the extent that Washington Irving may have written *A Tour on the Prairies* only to enhance his reputation as an American writer (after living in Europe for many years) by taking up a popular American subject—the West.

In the twentieth century the literature of the plains is more varied. There has been a major transition from the travel narrative to novels of settlement and the farm. This literature is also materialistic in that it deals with man's struggle to conquer or possess the land, to make it yield its material riches to him, to make the land serve him. Settling the land became a logical extension of the American dream, although the plains often proved inhospitable enough to alter the dream from the Garden of Eden to something less than that. The standard ingredients of the farm novel include the difficulties of pioneering, the struggle to make a living, the dangers and vagaries of the weather, drought and storm and grass fire, and always the hope that the next year will bring a better crop. In this hope the dream persisted. What must be kept in mind is that the dream was thoroughly materialistic, lowered to economic survival in hard times and raised to the accumulation of wealth in good times. However, it lacked the symbols of the mystic relationship between man and land, between man and nature. Roy W. Meyer, in *The Middle Western Farm Novel in the Twentieth Century*, suggests that this genre has functioned primarily to publicize farm life, "to the end that social and economic conditions may be improved."[10] In that respect there is little to distinguish one farm novel from another. Where noteworthy distinctions exist, they do not flow from originality or thematic significance as much as from memorable characters, as in Rølvaag's *Giants in the Earth* and Cather's *O Pioneers!* and *My Ántonia*. Nevertheless, a sense of propaganda, although variable in degree and kind, seems to underlie all the "farm novels," including the work of Hamlin Garland, Hyatt Downing, Lois Phillips Hudson, and even the more optimistic novels of Laura Ingalls Wilder.

When Rølvaag titled a chapter "The Great Plain Drinks the Blood of Christian Men and Is Satisfied," he was recognizing the land, or nature, as a formidable adversary that often caused Christian men to think in terms of "great desolation" and "utter darkness"—these words found in other chapter titles. Man and land are seen in opposition to each other, not joined in harmony; it should be remembered that opposition is a characteristic of a materialistic society. The use of personification allows Rølvaag to dramatize the opposition from the point of view of nature: "That night the Great Prairie stretched herself voluptuously; giantlike and full of cunning, she laughed softly into the reddish moon. 'Now we will see what human might may avail against us! . . . Now we'll see!' "[11] By implication, the Christian men's viewpoint is that the Great Plain (nature) is unfair, and they deserve something better than desolation and darkness. Furthermore, the reference to blood comes in the context of punishment and retribution rather than through any mystical relationship depending on blood as its metaphor. In the materialistic, realistic, naturalistic, or rational view, man is at odds with nature; he wants to conquer rather than join it, and so is separated from it except in an elementary physical relationship.[12]

The fiction and poetry of the Great Plains that centers upon the eastern edge of the region (bordering on, and dissolving into, prairie) is the least interested in, or susceptible to, any form of mysticism. What is often called an agricultural mysticism is probably more akin to a sense of place, an attachment to the land that helps to establish the identity of the people living on it. A sense of place is strongly felt in many farm novels and in the poetry of Ted Kooser, Greg Kuzma, and William Kloefkorn—to name a few—all of whom establish place by cataloguing ordinary things and describing the eccentricities of characters whose destiny is shaped by the place in a materialistic way. It seems that one must go farther west, more out in the open, before the direct confrontation with God and the land can occur. As Wallace Stegner has said, "I have felt . . . that in the middle of a great plain . . . a great dry, arid plain with the wind blowing the eyeballs out of your head and the grass all whistling and bending flat, you may feel small, but you don't feel unnoticed; you're out there with God. This is why a lot of people in the Bible went out into the wilderness, to consult their souls."[13]

In Frederick Manfred's *The Golden Bowl,* often identified as a farm novel, a mystical experience occurs when Maury temporarily abandons the farm on which he is staying and travels west to the Badlands. Here he senses the presence of the prehistoric dinosaurs and has a vision of the continuity of life, of man evolving from, and therefore being related to, creatures preceding him by an almost unthinkable time. Standing on the place where these creatures once lived, viewing their petrified bones, Maury feels a kinship with the older form of life, a kinship which then carries over to the people he meets on his journey. The unifying vision, which is mystical, is different from the sense of place he later discovers or achieves back on the farm at the end of his journey.[14]

A similar recognition of continuity, and therefore a kind of oneness, is felt by Cam Johnson, in Holger Cahill's *The Shadow of My Hand,* as he considers the gathering of bones on the plains. Years earlier, when the sodbusters were suffering from droughts and hard winters, they were paid ten dollars a ton for bones, mostly buffalo bones but also the bleached remains of cattle, antelope, Indians, and Indian fighters. The bones were shipped east and used to refine sugar, "and it seemed a shame that one might grind the remains of a forgotten hero to sweeten a cup of coffee."[15] The tone is not that of the enraptured or meditative mystic, but it suggests a strange communion.

These excursions from the materialistic atmosphere of the farm novel out into the "deeper" plains are brief and not totally convincing, but they are indications of a state of mind that becomes more common in American literature as it moves westward. Stegner observes: "I wouldn't be surprised if that sense of the immanence of deity, or force, or whatever it is you worship or fear in the universe, is felt more in a dry country than in a place where nature is essentially benign."[16] Wright Morris has said that "as the frontier moved westward, there was less and less of things, more and more of an inhospitable nature."[17] David Madden then finds an element of mysticism in Morris's concept of *things* as holy, but he sees another variety of this response farther west, away from the things of the social environment in a benign nature, where the plainsman is stripped down, "like the mystic," and feels both in and out of this world.[18]

The stripping down need not eliminate nature's own objects. They become the seen things that presumably can lead man to the unseen world. Mary Austin's *Land of Little Rain* is full of things of the desert and the mountains, but they are continually viewed in a condition of harmony, as though they are only parts of a single grand design that most people do not grasp. When, however, she attempts to reduce all ideas of the arid lands that I am including in a broad definition of the plains, she arrives at four terms: "beauty and madness and death and God." The materialist would approach these terms and the concepts for which they stand singly. He would recognize death as such, beauty as such, madness as such, and would probably have a rather narrow view of God apart from the other considerations.

For the mystic, however, with his unitary consciousness, any equation may be made from these elements, because all are essentially the same. Death and God may be identical; beauty and madness may be identical; just as God and beauty, or death and madness, may be the same things. This illustrates one of the big differences between Austin and Rølvaag: there is no beauty in Beret's madness, no beauty in Per Hansa's death, and while both are haunting and tragic, they seem to deny the existence of God.

To return to an earlier suggestion, I see the plains as a huge, spread-out fan with its handle to the East. There, literature is almost entirely materialistic in its approach to character and to nature; but as we move out toward the perimeter of the fan, where the plains not only meet the mountains but flow into them, the possibilities of mysticism seem to grow larger. The images of the plainsman and the mountain man become nearly indistinguishable. Population thins out in the mountains and elevation rises, but between two mountain ranges will be high plains, or plateaus, as well as valleys. The nearness to God on the open, sun-baked plains can only increase as man climbs higher to mesas, buttes, high deserts—land that in some ways extends the plains rather than shoring up their western end. It was at the juncture of mountain and plain that Frank Waters, perhaps our most mystical novelist, first encountered the materials of his life's work. In his semiautobiographical trilogy, recently published under the single title *Pike's Peak,* Rogier (a fictional version of Waters's maternal grandfather) walks out of Colorado Springs to a nearby mesa and hears the beat of Indian drums. It is like the beat of the earth, carrying into the bloodstream. "Suddenly and unconsciously, Rogier understood the spirit-Manitou, the place-spirit of the great western aridity that had made and kept him an exile in the land of his adoption."[19] Waters then stresses the timelessness of the rhythm, the insistence of it, and the earth-power that is absorbed through the legs of the dancers. Finally, he describes the result of this experience for Rogier, who now believes with his blood "more than the capacity of his mind could ever admit." Boné, one of the two characters in the trilogy representing Waters himself, has also witnessed the dance and has, even as a boy, "acknowledged the mystery of his creation"—"an ageless sound buried deep within the conscious self which reemerges dark and mysterious like a dream-flow of things unrecognizable, but still of that in us which reaffirms the lasting mystery of our creation."[20]

When Rogier abandons his job and goes into the mountains to search for gold, it is apparent that his so-called rational analysis of the situation is only a cover for his deep instinctual feeling that the veins of gold will lead "far down" into the depths where exists "that subterranean heart vibrating in unison with all eternal life." In other words, the heart of all life lies deep in the earth, beneath the mountain. Curiously, if the mountain is stripped away to its lowest depth, we are back on the level of the plains. The plains lie not only beneath the mountain but also over a prehistoric inland sea. The plains therefore have their own special quality and should be capable of evoking mystical experiences.

Wherever most western Indian tribes have settled, they have maintained a belief that certain mountains are sacred. The Sioux in South Dakota and Nebraska look to Harney's Peak, where Black Elk had his famous vision, or to Bear Butte. The Pueblos, who live near Frank Waters in northern New Mexico, look to Taos Mountain and, higher yet within adjoining mountains, the sacred Blue Lake. William Eastlake, in *Portrait of the Artist with Twenty-six Horses,* locates evil in a huge crack in the earth and sees the Indians striving upward, first to mesa, then to mountain, in order to die as near as possible to the Great Spirit of the sky and sun.[21]

Up to the present time, most mysticism in plains literature has come from the American Indian and what non-Indian writers have experienced of their religious beliefs and rituals. Walter Van Tilburg Clark, in *The Track of the Cat* (dismissed by most critics for its murky symbolism), compares the materialistic, visionary, and mystical views of life through four characters (three of them are brothers and the fourth is an Indian) who try to kill the black cat which has not only been killing cattle but has also taken on the dimensions of a mythical being. At the same time Clark is also examining the several types of men who followed their dreams into the West. Curt, most practical, safe in his belief that man can conquer nature, is eventually driven mad by the cat and runs blindly into a crevasse. His death is preceded by that of Arthur, the visionary, who does not see enough and is ambushed by the cat. The third brother, Hal, takes the irrational Indian, Joe Sam, with him on the hunt. His success seems to indicate that the ideal western American man is the one who can come to terms with the practical as well as the mystical. However, the cat he kills is not black, and the implication is that the black cat is a symbol of an eternal quality of life which man chooses to call "evil." Each man must come to a reckoning with such forces, just as Ahab required a reckoning with the whale.[22]

The mystic seeks the eternal moment, the unifying version, the timeless. Even in the West, where space is more important in most matters than time, illumination may come through the use of time. In *The Track of the Cat*, Harold finds the prints of a naked foot (Joe Sam's) in the snow and feels that the prints are not right; prints, dots and dashes, and lines left by animals were right, but not "this complicated, unique print." It was wrong. "There was too much time forgotten between."[23] That is, man has become separated from the creatures and has too often destroyed the unifying link between the natural world and the spiritual world. As Stegner reports in *Wolf Willow,* a pet deer led by the leash down Fifth Avenue in New York does not leave tracks.[24] The ironies in this fact go beyond the worlds of nature and spirit into a third world that is entirely of man's making, the world of steel and concrete, a city virtually without earth, where neither man nor animal can leave the kind of path that marks the passing of a creature, the existence of a man, the recognition of an identifiable life. Without tracks, without paths, without the naked foot in the snow, there is little to be remembered of individual lives. History requires such paths. Without them there is no record and therefore no immortality. Yet, as Waters suggests in *The Woman at Otowi Crossing,* the physical oneness sought by the atomic scientists at Los Alamos was not really different from the spiritual oneness understood by the Indians nearby for hundreds of years.[25]

Hayden Carruth has said that the prairie approaches Nirvana.[26] This is at the east end of the plains. Waters has said that the mountains hold the heart and secret of life. This is at the west end of the plains. Stegner then speaks for the plains themselves: "Eternity is a peneplain."[27] Stegner is not a mystic, but he is pointing, however inadvertently, toward a new literature of the plains, one that will move beyond the materialistic novel and poem of settlement, farm life, and small town characters to become a literature of awareness, influenced by the qualities of land that lead toward mysticism and supported at the base by an increasing sensitivity to the culture and visions of the American Indian. These visions are accessible to the perceptive writer who is willing to bridge that gap of "too much time forgotten between" modern man's drive toward materialistic success and earlier man's intimacy with nature. The landscape of the West, more than any other, encourages the spirit of man to renew meaningful contact with life's enduring mysteries.

NOTES

1. Jonathan Carver, *Travels Through the Interior Parts of North America in the Years 1766, 1767, and 1768* (1781; facsimile reprint ed., Minneapolis: Ross & Haines, 1956), pp. vii–viii.

2. Vardis Fisher, *Tale of Valor* (Garden City, New York: Doubleday, 1958), pp. 203–5.

3. Edwin James, *Account of an Expedition from Pittsburgh to the Rocky Mountains . . . of the U.S. Topographical Engineers* (1822–23; reprinted in Reuben G. Thwaites, ed., *Early Western Travels,* vols. 14–17, Cleveland: Arthur H. Clark Co., 1940–1907).

4. Josiah Gregg, *Commerce of the Prairies,* 2 vols. (1844; reprint ed., Philadelphia: J. B. Lippincott, 1962).

5. Lloyd McFarling, ed., *Exploring the Northern Plains* (Caldwell, Idaho: Caxton Printers, 1955), p. 183.

6. Washington Irving, *A Tour on the Prairies* (1835; reprint ed., *The Works of Washington Irving,* vol. 7, New York: Co-operative Publication Society, n.d.), p. 402.

7. Lewis Garrard, *Wah-to-yah and the Taos Trail* (1850; reprint ed., The Southwest Historical Series, vol. 6, Glendale, California: Arthur H. Clark Co., 1938), p. 185.

8. Ibid., p. 273.

9. Francis Parkman, *The Oregon Trail* (1849; reprint ed., New York: Random House, 1949), p. 59.

10. Roy W. Meyer, *The Middle Western Farm Novel in the Twentieth Century* (Lincoln: University of Nebraska Press, 1965), p. 199.

11. O. E. Rölvaag, *Giants in the Earth* (1927; reprint ed., New York: Harper & Row, 1965), p. 349.

12. D. H. Lawrence and Frank Waters, emphasizing unity and intuition rather than conflict and opposition, speak of the "belief of the blood," a nonrational mode of thought. That such a notion should

appear more often in the Southwest than in the North may be attributed in part to intimacy with Indian perceptions but also, perhaps, to the softer climate, which, under some circumstances, alleviates the harshness of the land and allows time for man to contemplate the mysteries of nature. In northern fiction, survival seems to be the major theme.

13. Wallace Stegner, "Interview," *The Great Lakes Review* 2 (Summer 1975): 12.

14. Frederick Manfred, *The Golden Bowl* (St. Paul, Minn.: Webb Publishing Co., 1944).

15. Holger Cahill, *The Shadow of My Hand* (New York: Harcourt, Brace, 1956), p. 65.

16. Stegner, "Interview," p. 12.

17. Wright Morris, "Interview," *Great Lakes Review* 1 (Winter 1975): 5.

18. David Madden, *Wright Morris* (New York: Twayne, 1964), p. 71.

19. Frank Waters, *The Wild Earth's Nobility* (New York: Liveright, 1935), p. 191. This novel was incorporated into *Pike's Peak* (Chicago: Swallow Press, 1971), where the wording of the passage quoted is different, p. 111.

20. Ibid., p. 193. The passage is worded differently in *Pike's Peak,* p. 112.

21. William Eastlake, *Portrait of the Artist with Twenty-Six Horses* (New York: Simon and Schuster, 1938).

22. Walter Van Tilburg Clark, *The Track of the Cat* (New York: Random House, 1949).

23. Ibid., pp. 156, 157.

24. Wallace Stegner, *Wolf Willow: A History, a Story, and a Memory of the Last Plains Frontier* (New York: Viking, 1962), p. 273.

25. Frank Waters, *The Woman at Otowi Crossing* (Denver: Alan Swallow, 1966).

26. Hayden Carruth, "South Dakota: State without End," *Nation,* 24 January 1923, pp. 87–90.

27. Stegner, *Wolf Willow,* p. 7.

BARBARA HOWARD MELDRUM

Agrarian versus Frontiersman
in Midwestern Fiction

OUR AMERICAN CONCEPTION of the West has been dominated by two cultural myths, the myth of the garden and the myth of the western hero.[1] Identified with the first is the figure of the American farmer; with the second, the frontiersman. Each of these figures is associated with a cluster of values we tend to link with the settlement of the western frontier. The agrarian life is supposed to ennoble man, encouraging the dignity and self-respect that come from self-sufficiency and discouraging the corruption of morals that comes from a metropolitan environment and an industrial economy. Jefferson calls the laborers of the soil the chosen people of God, and Crèvecoeur praises the American farmer for his industry, independence, domestic commitment, and his contribution to a growing national economy.[2] The frontiersman plays an essential role in opening up new western lands for settlement; this task of trailblazing and pioneering is seen as an indispensable part of the cycle of western development even by critics, such as Crèvecoeur, who condemn the character of the frontiersman. Those who view the frontiersman more positively praise his heroism, his freedom, independence, adventurousness—his assertion of self above man-made laws.

44

In the saga of western settlement man returns to a primitive state where he is removed from an eastern or European civilization and is dependent upon nature for his survival. Frederick Jackson Turner, in his classic essay on the frontier, claims that this primitivism leads to a "perennial rebirth" which fosters the development of a distinctively American character, marked by its individualism, resourcefulness, and sense of freedom. The existence of free land is required for this development, and Turner believes an agrarian economy will best foster American democracy. He affirms a unified ideal wherein the best traits of frontiersman and agrarian are combined and are attainable through the cyclical experience which occurs when one is "reborn" on the frontier and passes through the primitive to the civilized stage of development.[3]

Many American writers have not been as positive as Turner about the ways the western environment affects human fulfillment. Defeat and disillusionment haunt the characters of western fiction when the better life they seek so often eludes them or proves to be a hollow achievement. The reasons for defeat are various and often complicated. Some light can, I believe, be shed on the nature of their defeat by examining the interrelationships of agrarian and frontiersman traits and values. The western farmer seeks individual fulfillment in a way of life that obviously demands close ties to the land. But he is not pure agrarian; he is usually a blend of the agrarian and the frontiersman, and the frontiersman traits frequently promote exploitation of the land and domination of other people. Moreover, the agrarian ideal of home, family, and prosperity often leads to a spiritually unfulfilling materialism.

We can see these connections in representative novels of three midwestern writers who focus on farm families of immigrant background. The first, Ole Rølvaag's *Giants in the Earth* (1927), presents the pioneering experience of sodbreaking settlers. The second, Sophus Keith Winther's Grimsen trilogy (1936–38), portrays Danish immigrants who begin as tenant farmers and who never attain freedom from landlord or mortgage-holder. The third, Frederick Manfred's

This Is the Year (1947), dramatizes the aspirations and failures of the son of an immigrant pioneer.[4]

Rølvaag's Per Hansa is both frontiersman and agrarian; his achievements and his failures emerge from the duality of his own character. Like Crèvecoeur's new American, he has come to the New World to realize a dream of freedom, independence, and prosperity, and he seeks to achieve its fulfillment through farm labor on his own land. Like Turner's mythical frontiersman, he returns to primitive conditions and struggles with natural forces as he seeks to transform the "Endless Wilderness . . . into a habitable land for human beings" (p. 287). His dream is a fairy tale of a new kingdom of independence, individual dignity, and material abundance. He wants to share this dream with his wife, Beret, but the agonizing truth slowly emerges that she cannot share his dream because she can "never be like him" (p. 221). He, like so many others, has been stricken with "the west-fever"; like other adventurers, he has believed that movement westward would bring him to the Promised Land. But Beret calls that west-fever a plague (p. 219), and perhaps it is a more subtle, insidious plague than the locusts that often devastated the settlers during their early years of sod-breaking. The west-fever calls forth the frontiersman traits, and these traits do not always promote agrarian values.

The novel focuses on two conflicts: the first is the pioneer's struggle to master the environment and in so doing to wrest material success from the resources of nature; the second is the conflict between Per Hansa and Beret. These conflicts overlap, for marital tensions emerge and are fostered by Beret's difficulties in adjusting to the barren, primitive, uncivilized life on the prairie and by Per Hansa's absorption in the challenging tasks of pioneering. Per Hansa's frontiersman traits plus good luck usually enable him to succeed in his struggle with nature, and, curiously, although Per Hansa is a farmer, the memorable scenes do not focus on farming experiences but on what could be called frontiersman adventures. Often these episodes also contribute to marital tensions. In the opening chapter Per Hansa discovers the trail of his comrades through some rather astute tracking in the darkness of night (a feat that surely rivals some of Leatherstocking's exploits). But his self-assurance and desire to protect his wife have kept him from sharing his concern when they were lost; his masculine overprotectiveness contributes to their marital difficulties. Later, Per Hansa courageously meets the Indians who camp nearby and wins a pony by applying skills he had learned as a fisherman to an Indian suffering from blood poisoning. But his taunts before the frightened women and children of the settlement "coarsen" him in Beret's eyes and she reprimands him publicly for the first time in their many years of marriage (p. 70). Other exploits also are those of the frontiersman more than the farmer: Per Hansa is the only one who can be depended on to find the lost cows; he devises an ingenious scheme for trapping ducks; he trades furs with the Indians not simply to augment family income but to get away from the confines of winter homelife and pursue adventure; and he makes his way through a snowstorm by keeping before him an image of western conquest as he pushes onward toward the Rocky Mountains, even though he is actually traveling east rather than west (pp. 255, 265). Even his early sowing of wheat stems more from frontiersman than agrarian traits; this neophyte farmer is impatient and reckless, gambling against great odds in the manner of the Forty-niner Adventurer Frank Norris describes in *The Octopus*.[5]

Perhaps the conflict between frontiersman and agrarian traits is best seen when Per Hansa discovers stakes with strange names on them, indicating that others have laid claim to the property his neighbors thought was theirs. Beret's premonitions are correct when she recalls the tales she has heard "of how people in this wild country would ruthlessly take the matters of law and justice into their own hands" (pp. 122–23); Per Hansa recognizes that even if the law is on his friend's side, the law is too far away, and thus these claimants may try to take the land by force (p. 137). Indeed they do; but Hans Olsa's powerful body is equal to the challenge: he strikes down the challenger who has threatened him with a sledgehammer, picks up the man, and hurls him "over the heads of the crowd," where he crashes into a wagon (p. 143). Beret is deeply disturbed by Per Hansa's behavior: he has removed stakes that were sanctioned by Old World tradition as sacred landmarks. Even when she learns that the stakes were illegally placed, she is not comforted: "Would he have done any different" if they had been legal? She believes that "this desolation out here called forth all that was evil in human nature." Although the opportunities for free land seem to be limitless, people seek by "deceit and force" to make their own way and to satisfy their greed. The crowning blow comes for Beret when she hears her husband tell his friends, "in a loud voice, with boisterous, care-free zest," how he had found the stakes and had destroyed them. Again Beret reprimands Per Hansa before the others for taking pride in an act that would have been "a shameful sin" in the old country. When he retorts that the easiest, simplest way to cope with such difficulties is to "kick the dog that bites you," Beret replies that such a code is "poor Christianity" and cautions, "We'd better take care lest we all turn into beasts and savages out here!" (pp. 148–50). Turner's notion of a perennial rebirth in the western wilderness takes on somber dimensions in Rølvaag's novel. The structure of this chapter underscores the sinister implications. It begins with Per Hansa's romantic fairy-tale vision of fulfillment of his agrarian dreams as his restless blood pushes him onward "toward the wonders of the future" made possible by "endless" rich soil (pp. 107–9) and it ends with Beret's reprimand and a marital rift (p. 150).

This episode prompts Beret to see her husband with new eyes. "Was this the person in whom she had believed no evil could dwell?" (p. 148). Beret's religious views may be dogmatically narrow, even inseparable from her psychotic behavior; but if she is a "clinical case," she is, as Robert Scholes has pointed out, "a case like Cassandra, and the fires of prophetic truth shine through her madness."[6] She sees sin in their prairie life: here where "Earth takes us" (p. 432) man has no time to think of God, only of self and pressing material needs. Hans Olsa lies on his deathbed after valiantly struggling to protect his cattle from a blizzard; but his concerns were primarily material ones, as he recognized that failure

would make him "a considerably poorer man" (p. 419), and
Beret's admonition to Per Hansa rings true: "You know what
our life has been: land and houses, and then more land, and
cattle! . . . Can't you understand that a human being ever
becomes concerned over his sins and wants to be freed from
them?" (p. 442). When Per Hansa continues to resist her
efforts to get him to go for the minister, she wonders, "Had he
become stone blind?" (p. 446). Beret has become obsessed
with sin—her own and others—and she has prayed fervently
for her husband (p. 441); but he never sees with her eyes, and
in the final image of the book his vacant eyes face, in death,
the west which has been the impetus of his fairy-tale vision of
the future. In hope he had named his son Peder Victorious;
but Beret had cried out against that name: "How can a man
be *victorious* out here, where the evil one gets us all! " (p. 368).
It is true that the minister assures Beret that the name is not
blasphemous, and in the sequel to this novel, the minister
urges Beret to "learn to find the good in your fellow man."[7]
But extreme though Beret's views may be, she has prophetic
vision: she knows that the land takes not only their lives but
their souls, and her gloomy vision is confirmed in Peder's
ironic destiny.

Per Hansa is a giant, a western frontiersman who performs mighty deeds of valor to found an agrarian kingdom for
his sons. He shares the frontier spirit which declared that
"everything was possible" on that "endless plain"—"there
was no such thing as the Impossible any more" (pp. 414, 241,
414-15). But during a blizzard that is likened to Noah's flood,
which was sent by God to purge the earth of sinners, Per
Hansa is forced out to his death by his dearest friends and by
his wife, who have come to believe that Per Hansa can do the
impossible.[8] Per Hansa knows full well the perils of nature,
and he has also learned his own limitations as a human
being; but he is a victim of the reckless western spirit he has
helped to promote and seems to embody. The very traits that
have helped him so often to overcome difficulties now con-
spire to thrust him out into the awful solitude of the snow-
swept prairie. His death comes from physical causes, but is
emblematic of the prairie solitude as "a form of freedom"

which some cannot endure (p. 363). He is frozen in the posture of one resting before pressing onward toward the west; but his rotting corpse, anachronistically clad in warm clothes when discovered in the warmth of May, suggests a purpose that has gone sour.

Rølvaag's novel focuses on the pioneering farmer, a frontiersman claiming free land in the western wilderness. Winther's Grimsen trilogy also portrays immigrants inspired by a western vision of free land, independence, and prosperity (1:3). But these Danish immigrants arrive in the 1890s, when, as Turner points out, the frontier has closed. There is no free land, and the Grimsens must rent a rundown farm and struggle not only with nature but with an economic system that keeps them in perpetual subjugation no matter how hard they may work. In such a context the frontiersman traits seem to recede and the agrarian concerns are foremost.

The Grimsens come to America seeking a better way of life. But true to the pattern of development in the American West, they undergo a reversion to primitive living. This primitivism is not, however, the return to nature attended by a perennial rebirth that Turner spoke of; rather, it is a primitivism of poverty and cultural alienation. They have left a comfortable home in Denmark but now find themselves in an unpainted, tumbledown house that looks "more like a chicken house than a human dwelling place" (1:18). Meta struggles to bring the values of the civilization she knows into this house, but is continually frustrated by crushing poverty. Although she cleans away the accumulated filth, her patches on the deteriorating walls only partially conceal the gaping holes, and her efforts to put up wallpaper are doomed to failure when the paper refuses to stick to the rotten walls. She plans a baptismal service for her young daughter, seeking to follow the religious traditions of her past; to prepare for the minister's visit, she persuades Peter to buy a porcelain wash basin, pitcher, and pot so that their home "will look a little bit civilized" (1:32). Her materialistic goals are necessarily extremely limited by the poverty the family endures, but there is no doubt about the nature of her aspirations as she seeks to achieve some measure of comfort and beauty in their home.

Peter's materialism is of another sort. While not opposed to Meta's more feminine concern for their dwelling, he invests in possessions that will promote his farmwork. Even though he knows that he cannot take permanent improvements with him if he should leave his rented farm, he invests in them anyway to facilitate his work and to increase his chances for profit. Although he seems to be improving his condition, he is actually developing the farm for his landlord. When the day comes that he must lose the farm, he realizes he has spared himself little but has done virtually nothing to improve the inside of the house. Like Per Hansa, he seeks development of his land as a means to achieve family stability and well-being—agrarian values, but they are asserted in ways that seem to neglect his wife and family. Paradoxically, the male agrarian's materialism derives from feminine values of home, family, and prosperity; but these ends are sought in ways that often deny the very goals they seek to validate.

In spite of continued frustrations and disappointments precipitated by economic conditions, the Grimsens do exemplify positive agrarian values in their way of life. Although cash may be in scarce supply, they never lack for food, and the abundance of nature seems to promote a sense of security and well-being. Moreover, when nature is uncooperative and crops are disappointing, these people recognize and accept the fluctuations of nature because the "battle with the elements" is one they can understand; it is the "invisible foe" of the economic system which finally conquers them (3:247; see also 1:279). Their work with the soil may be wearing to the body and financially unrewarding, yet it is valuable discipline and is honorable. Even when threatened with economic ruin, Peter will not allow his sons to work in a stone quarry; such work would be beneath the dignity of a farmer (3:186–87). The title of the third volume of the trilogy, *This Passion Never Dies,* refers to the passion for the land—Peter's Old World peasant heritage which first drew him to America in search of the Promised Land and which is the legacy he

passes on to his sons. All but one of his sons leave the land for
other vocations; but they carry with them the values their
farm life has nurtured. When Hans's American wife charges
that he is like all the Danes—"You don't want a wife, you
want a kitchen slave"—he relates the value of work to
American development: "If I know anything about American
history, of what Americans have had to do to turn a wilderness into a civilized nation, then the Danes I know are more
truly American than you and your kind" (3:96–97).[9] The
Grimsens may not have achieved the realization of their
dreams, since America promises more than it gives (3:234);
but, like Crèvecoeur's farmers, they have acted in response to
values that are associated with agrarian life and in so doing
they have also affirmed their identity as Americans.[10]

Frontiersman traits also undergird the Grimsens' agrarian values. Both Peter and Meta emigrated as courageous
individuals willing to face the uncertainties of life in a new
land (see 3:234, 260). Peter is especially attracted by a country that provides "scope for a man" (1:27). He is challenged by
the "possibilities for the future" (1:279), an American future
that seems to demand severance from a European past. In
typical frontier fashion, the past is left behind—by action if
not by sentiment. As Peter and Meta discover, "While they
had been facing east in their dreams their thoughts and
actions had been turned west, until now they were a part of
the new world" (1:305). "Our thoughts go back, but our hands
work here" (3:233). Although this new country seems to demand some sort of repudiation of the past, the antiintellec-
tualism of the westward, future-oriented, self-indulgent
frontiersman seems to be lacking.[11] Both Rølvaag and
Winther write of first-generation emigrants who possess the
courage and love of freedom of the western pioneer, but who
still cling in important ways to Old World culture and consequently establish some sense of continuity in the transition
from Old World civilization to New World primitive frontier
and American identity.

Another aspect of the frontiersman influence can be seen
in the Grimsen boys' fascination with the western mythology
of the nickel novels. Not only are they avid readers, but they

act out the tales in play, adopting the roles of their heroes and inventing their own adventures. In true western fashion, they take the law into their own hands as they fantasize the lynching of their family's enemy, the loan shark Jacob Paulson. But their fantasy of lawless freedom and individualistic justice culminates in sadism when they begin to torment a stray dog, then finally kill it in wanton violence (1:108–17). This orgy of misdirected assertiveness is later paralleled by a real-life escapade in which the pupils of the country school are led by the Grimsen boys to revolt against a tyrannical schoolmarm. Their revolt is conceived in a desire for justice that is not forthcoming within the system; by taking matters into their own hands they succeed in freeing themselves from the teacher, but their revolt gets out of control as revenge twists justice into excessive violence and a destructiveness which harms even themselves (1:150–62). These echoes of frontierism suggest the sinister side of the western hero myth; but the positive side is also present. The young Hans finds it useful to identify with Buffalo Bill when he needs courage to brave the night fears that plague him while carrying out an errand (1:224). Years later, when as a young man he faces a seemingly impossible task, his brother calls him by the name of one of his nickel-novel heroes, and this association gives Hans the confidence he needs (3:268). Before his mission is accomplished, his confidence needs further bolstering, and this time the inspiration comes from memories of his father, who had inspired him with the same courage and determination that had enabled him to emigrate and to pursue his goals with unflagging determination (3:227). In Peter the agrarian and the frontiersman meet in concord as the positive traits complement and reinforce each other. Winther's trilogy thereby enunciates the American ideal of progress through an affirmation of the western spirit.

Winther comes the closest of these three writers to portraying the achievement of the American dream through a Turnerian view of western development. However, the positive resolution of the tale pertains to the son rather than to the father; Peter Grimsen is defeated when he loses the farm he had sought to make his own for so many years. The sources of his defeat lie not within himself, but outside the self in a socioeconomic system that leaves him helpless. The fact that this trilogy was written in the 1930s by a confirmed naturalist no doubt does much to explain the portrayal of Peter's destiny.[12] Even though the frontiersman-agrarian traits and values may coexist in a harmonious balance within the Grimsen family, Peter suffers defeat. But we can, I believe, see evidence of a destructive imbalance in the people through whom the external economic forces act upon Peter. Jacob Paulson is another Danish immigrant, but one who early learns to live off the misfortunes of others by becoming a moneylender and mortgage-holder. He and others like him become land-hungry; their greed leads to overextension; although ultimately defeated, they bring down with them the honest, hard-working farmers like Peter Grimsen. Arthur Moore, in his study of the frontier mind, claims that greed is a form of economic anxiety which emerges on the frontier when the expectation of an "Earthly Paradise" is frustrated by the disappointing realities of frontier life.[13] In Winther's fiction an avariciousness born of the frontier experience leads indirectly to Peter Grimsen's defeat.

The sources of failure are again internalized when we turn to Frederick Manfred's *This Is the Year.* Of the three authors considered here, Manfred provides the most intensive examination of man's relationship to the land itself, revealing that the life of the farmer does not necessarily lead to the positive character traits we have come to associate with agrarianism. The protagonist, Pier Frixen, never wavers in his commitment to farming and he does love the land. But he doesn't know *how* to love the land. Similarly, he doesn't know *how* to love his wife. Manfred has carefully interwoven the elements of his tale by equating the land with woman so that marriage to woman parallels "marriage" to the land as Pier takes over his father's farm; productivity and barrenness of farm and family coincide; and failure to his wife corresponds with his failure to the land. Moreover, the reasons for failure are the same in both realms, and they are rooted in Pier's frontiersman traits.

Pier's father was a Frisian immigrant pioneer, home-

steading in the northwest corner of Iowa. Pier was named for
a Frisian hero, Great Pier, a fighter for Frisian freedom.
Other allusions to Frisian legendary history link Pier to a
glorious past of valiant conquest. Frank Norris once wrote
that the westward frontier movement began when the Frisians invaded Britain—the "Wild West . . . of that century."[14] If so, then the Frisians were the first frontiersmen,
and Pier is their twentieth-century agrarian descendant, a
man who thrills to the battles and gambles of farm life (p.
300). He is true to his heritage in his consistent desire for
freedom, his stubborn independence, and his reliance on
physical prowess. Both Pier and his father show little respect
for the law as they illegally seine fish in the Sioux River, and
Pier resists what he calls government interference when his
cattle must be inspected for tuberculosis. His rugged individualism will respond to a neighbor in distress, as is shown
when he fights to rescue a neighbor from foreclosure; but that
same individualism keeps him from listening to the advice of
Pederson, the county extension agent, and from accepting
government price supports that might prevent (or at least
delay) foreclosure on his own farm. Pier is a dogged fighter
and thereby wins the respect of even his enemies (see p. 590).
But determination, fortitude, self-assertion, and a fighting
spirit cannot ward off persistent drought and its economic
consequences. Indeed, these traits prompt Pier to pursue a
single direction without regard for alternatives, and that
single-mindedness hastens his defeat.

Pier's son, Teo, sums up his father's problem succinctly
when he says, "You never stop to think things out. You rush
into things too much. You figure everything's got to be done
in a hurry. By bullin' it through. Maybe that was all right in
old pioneer days. But not now" (p. 575). Pier is an exploiting
frontiersman who takes all he can get and pushes his way
with bullish power. He may love the land, but he doesn't
know how to treat the land so that it will respond bountifully,
just as he loves his wife Nertha but doesn't know how to
express that love in ways that will nurture and preserve it.
He rapes his wife as he rapes the land. Nertha, who is named
for the goddess of earth, bears but one son, then in spite of

Pier's desire for more sons deliberately miscarries to avoid bringing another son under her husband's domination. She ages prematurely, becoming a worn-out, unattractive, nagging woman. So also does the earth respond to Pier's bulling ways. Because he plows uphill and downhill instead of contouring, erosion creates a gully that eventually eats away at the foundation of his home. Because he overtills the land, he turns it into dust to be blown away by the wind or washed away by rain. He never learns what the land is really like, never makes himself fit the land; instead, he tries to make the land fit him (p. 574).

The only adaptability Pier consistently demonstrates is an ingenuity that gets him out of several tight spots when his will to survive dominates. On three occasions Pier nearly falls to his death. First, he slips and falls from the peak of his barn roof after repairing the cupola. When his efforts to grasp the cleats fail and he realizes he can't stop the fall, he turns over and over on the sloping roof so that he will land in the manure pile instead of on the hard earth. The plunge into the soggy manure is a kind of baptism; he has been daydreaming about another woman and he feels that "this green soup, this stink, made up for, canceled out, the sin of dreaming about Kaia. The manure had washed his sins away" (p. 121). Presumably reborn in innocence, he does not seem to learn from his experience; and his "baptism" does not make him a better husband. Years later he climbs up his windmill to unjam it, but the weathered ladder rungs give way so that he cannot find a solid hold. Again he uses his wits, realizes that a fall straight down will break his body on the widening uprights, and decides to leap away from the windmill. His mind conjures up a western image of Indians falling from ponies, somersaulting and avoiding injury. "He was sure of himself. He had a plan." In his somersaulting roll his legs absorb some of the shock, then spring out like grasshopper legs and thrust him forward. His nose is shattered; otherwise he escapes serious injury (p. 238).

Since both falls occur while Pier is performing necessary farming tasks that require grit and daring, Manfred may be suggesting some of the heroic aspects of a farmer's life. It takes a real man to scale those heights, and it takes a resilient, ingenious man to survive the perils that could so easily lead to death. But Pier's third fall does not occur in the course of his agrarian duties. His wife has just died after wasting away in mind and body, and Pier is consumed by guilt because he feels responsible for her death. He wanders out to Devil's Gulch, stares at the water beneath him, fascinated by how easy it would be to die—just a slip of the foot—and he falls, plunging into the dark waters. Instead of surrendering to death, his will to survive reasserts itself; he struggles against the undertow and thrusts himself up into the air. He has descended into a "great watery womb" and has been reborn (pp. 503–5). Yet this rebirth does not lead to a new life. The reasons why Pier's rebirths are abortive are suggested by the complex symbolism of Devil's Gulch.

The gulch lies near Nertha's family home; some of her happiest memories are of wandering in the fields near the gulch, picking wild flowers and herbs. These flowers, though, are beyond the gulch, and Nertha is prepubescent (p. 283). The gulch, with its red lips, its slash in the earth, is identified with woman. When Nertha tells Pier she is pregnant, the image he immediately sees is Devil's Gulch (p. 233); when Pier falls into the waters of the gulch, he has entered a womb. But the womb becomes a grave; it is the devil's gulch, and the only exit from the abyss is to scale the Devil's Stairway (p. 505). The gulch is to Pier "the mouth of a toothless, bloody-gummed monster" (p. 111); when he falls from the windmill he sees "black death below. It grinned up at him. It was as distinct as the red-gummed laugh of Devil's Gulch" (p. 237). The sexuality suggested by the gulch is fraught with possibilities for life and death, fertility and barrenness, like the earth which Pier also seeks to know and to master.[15] Pier is drawn to the earth by a gravitational force both physical and spiritual. The same earth that can respond with bountiful crops can also break his body.

Although Pier has the physical resilience to survive his encounters with earth, he lacks an inward development that would teach him how to love. Pederson tells Pier, "With just a little more sense you'd make a perfect fit. It takes a hero to

live out here. . . . Where have you ever seen country with
bigger ups and downs than this here God's country? . . . It
takes a hero to survive such stuff. A hero who thinks" (pp.
604–5). Pier does not "think." While he begins to see where he
has gone awry, he lacks the ability to pull it all together and
chart new, positive directions. He has survived each encounter with death, and he survives the loss of his farm with
typical resilience—"I'm a young buck yit. My heart's still
green," he says, as he leaves the farm he has ruined by his
stubbornly exploiting farming methods. Pier, though, has
been reborn before, without gaining greater wisdom. He
hasn't really changed.[16] He moves out into space, looking for
another place, another life. He sings the same song he had
sung when the tale began with his wedding day. The first
chapter was titled "The Promised Land," and the last chapter
is "God's Country." The Promised Land Pier had sought
through his marriage to Nertha and to the land has not been
found. He carries in his suitcase the biblical placard Nertha
had brought to their home: "The *EARTH* is the *LORD'S* and
the *FULLNESS THEREOF*" (p. 613). Pier never fully
realizes the ways in which that land belongs to God. As he
once possessed Nertha physically but realized how little he
knew her and how limited was his ability to possess her (p.
61), so he has sought to possess the land but has never really
known it and has failed to make it his. Like Guthrie's Boone
Caudill in *The Big Sky* (1947), he has ruined his paradise, has
destroyed what he loved most, and he has no place to go.

   Pier fails because he cannot integrate the frontiersman
and the agrarian within himself. As he stands pondering his
fate, he tries to understand what has happened:

> Why hadn't he and the land been able to get along? Why? Pier
> lifted the massive question in his mind and turned the long bole
> of it over. Why?
> He had loved Siouxland. He had wanted it. He had tried to tie
> himself to an alien past, to the old Mound Builders, to the
> Sioux, to the heroes Jesse James and Buckskin Teddy. To
> Cyclops and Ulysses even. What was wrong?
> Ae, he had tried to catch his anchor into the soils, had tried to
> get his roots down so deep that neither the wind nor flood, heat

nor cold, could ever tear him out again . . . and had failed.
Did a man have to die before he became a part of the old lady
earth? Did a man's land work easier after it had been sweetened
with the dust of his blood and brains?
Pier stood up and shivered. Life was a double task here on the
new prairies. A man had to fight the Alde Han, the elements; a
man had to get his roots into the soil, earn his birthright. A
double task. Ae. [P. 611; ellipses are Manfred's]

Pier is not equal to the double task. Instead, he is split,
divided. He has sought to dissociate himself from his Frisian
past in an effort to be truly American.[17] In the process he has
lost the sense of family identity and continuity that would
prompt him to treat his aged parents with respect and affec-
tion. His efforts to identify with the heroes of the past come
too late; he is alien, alone. As he wanders through the empty
rooms of his home for the last time, the ground gives beneath
him; the erosion he has failed to check breaks the house
asunder. Walking away from the house, he turns for one last
look; the house his father had built "lay cleavered beneath
the skies" (p. 614).[18] So ends the pioneer's dream. Like Poe's
House of Usher, the house of Frixen is sinking, reclaimed by
the earth. Pier leaves, singing defiantly. He is resilient, and
he survives; but his endurance is not the sort that will help
him ultimately to prevail. His is but a Pyrrhic victory.[19]

These three writers, Rølvaag, Winther, and Manfred,
have addressed in various ways the relationship between
man and the earth in the context of a pioneering midwestern
American experience. They all share in affirming an agrarian love for the land; yet none portrays a clearly victorious
ending. Indeed, in various ways, each points toward alienation from the land. The most optimistic of the three, Winther,
shows that the values of the father can be passed on to the son,
but the son will not work out his destiny on the land, and the
bitter struggles of his parents so shape his own vision that he
plans to leave the Midwest in search of a new life farther west
(3:265). Per Hansa's son, Peder, may remain for a time on the
family farm; but both his marriage and his hopes for a political role in the destiny of his agrarian region are shattered;[20]
like Manfred's Pier, he really has no place to go. All these

male protagonists experience defeat. Except for Winther's Meta, their wives seem to thwart the realization of their dreams and contribute to their fate. Failures with the land are paralleled by failures in love.

These writers also join in affirming a western frontier spirit—a spirit of rugged individualism marked by courage, fortitude, and love of freedom. Here, however, the consequences are far more ambivalent, for freedom can mean alienation, solitude, and a false assumption of limitless possibilities. A frontier psychology assumes that one can always go someplace else; failure can be blamed on circumstances—an economic system, the weather, other people; the rugged individual can pick himself up and begin again elsewhere. Yet what happens if there is no place to go? One can argue endlessly the pros and cons of Turner's frontier thesis. Undoubtedly it is simplistic. But whether one juggles with dates and places, as Walter Prescott Webb and others have done; or whether one uses a mythical perspective, as Robin Winks does when he says that some countries have appropriated a frontier concept because they needed it—however one turns the question, there does seem to be something valid in the thesis: we once had a frontier, and we don't have it now. With our shift away from frontierism come new ways of looking at the individual. Freud believed that we are creatures of instinct, driven to seek pleasure and thwarted by the limitations civilization places on our attempts to achieve self-fulfillment. His theories are similar to the frontier psychology I have been describing—which is no surprise if we take seriously Webb's thesis of a four-hundred-year frontier era, from the Renaissance to about 1900, in which America was the frontier of Europe.[21] This age was distinguished by the great importance placed on the individual. Now, however, the frontier era is past, and newer psychological theories attempt to chart directions for a frontierless era.[22]

Rølvaag, Winther, and Manfred write from a frontier perspective. Yet they all see that physical conquest and movement in space are not necessarily modes of victory. Each writer in various ways makes us look inward for the source of and the solution to our problems. In so doing, they point the way for individual growth in a frontierless era.

NOTES

1. Henry Nash Smith defined and described these myths in his pioneering study, *Virgin Land: The American West as Symbol and Myth* (Cambridge: Harvard University Press, 1950). Other critics have built upon Smith's work. For a recent study of the two conflicting myths see Jay Gurian, *Western American Writing: Tradition and Promise* (De Land, Florida: Everett / Edwards, 1975).

2. See Thomas Jefferson, *Notes on the State of Virginia*, Query 19, and J. Hector St. John de Crèvecoeur, *Letters from an American Farmer*, Letter 3.

3. Frederick Jackson Turner, "The Significance of the Frontier in American History" (1893), in *The Frontier in American History*, ed. Ray A. Billington (New York: Holt, Rinehart, and Winston, 1962), pp. 2–4, 37.

4. References, cited in the text, are to the following: O. E. Rölvaag, *Giants in the Earth* (1927; reprint ed., New York: Harper & Row, 1965); Sophus Keith Winther, *Take All to Nebraska* (1937; reprint ed., Lincoln: University of Nebraska Press, 1976), *Mortgage Your Heart* (New York: Macmillan, 1937), *This Passion Never Dies* (New York: Macmillan, 1938) (volume numbers refer to the novels in order of publication); and Feike Feikema [Frederick Manfred], *This Is the Year* (Garden City, N. Y.: Doubleday, 1947).

5. *Complete Works of Frank Norris* (Port Washington, N. Y.: Kennikat Press, 1967), 2:14. See also Norris's essay, " 'The Literature of the West': A Reply to W. R. Lighton," in *Literary Criticism of Frank Norris*, ed. Donald Pizer (Austin: University of Texas Press, 1964), pp. 104–7. Per Hansa does differ somewhat from the exploiting Adventurers of Norris: unlike them, he has a love for the land and does not consciously exploit it.

6. Robert Scholes, "The Fictional Heart of the Country: From Rølvaag to Gass," in *Ole Rølvaag: Artist and Cultural Leader*, ed. Gerald Thorson (Northfield, Minn.: St. Olaf College Press, 1975), p. 3.

7. O. E. Rölvaag, *Peder Victorious* (1929; reprint ed., New York: Harper & Row, 1966), p. 169.

8. See pp. 443, 445, 451. Beret, less optimistic than Hans Olsa and Sorine, maintains that God will forgive if one tries to do the impossible but fails. She does, however, seem to be reasonably

confident that Per Hansa can do the "impossible"; her attitude contrasts dramatically with her earlier resentment when others urged Per Hansa to do things for them which they felt only he could do.

9. For other affirmations of agrarian values, see 3:232, 271.

10. For further discussion of the Americanization of the Grimsens, see my essay, "Duality and the Dream in S. K. Winther's Grimsen Trilogy," *Prairie Schooner* 49 (Winter 1975–76): 311–19.

11. For a provocative study of the frontiersman character with emphasis on the negative traits, see Arthur K. Moore, *The Frontier Mind: A Cultural Analysis of the Kentucky Frontiersman* (Lexington: University of Kentucky Press, 1957).

12. Winther has affirmed a naturalistic philosophy in many conversations, lectures, and letters. He carefully explicates the relevance of determinism to tragic drama in his *Eugene O'Neill: A Critical Study* (New York: Random House, 1934), and Desmond Powell has noted that Winther's naturalistic philosophy gives unity to his fiction in "Sophus Winther: The Grimsen Trilogy," *American-Scandinavian Review* 36 (June 1948): 144–47.

13. Moore, *The Frontier Mind*, pp. 23–29.

14. Norris, "The Frontier Gone at Last," in *Literary Criticism of Frank Norris*, p. 111.

15. Cf. p. 54: "The country had been full of evil. It had not made men prosperous or happy. . . . The Land was a woman, treacherous, touched, bewitched."

16. Manfred has said of Pier: "He learns the lesson that you have to become a piece of the earth. Son of the earth. Not a destroyer of the earth. A son of the earth. Like a son loves his mother. You have to live with it and love it and protect it. . . . He isn't a lover of [the earth or his wife] until it is almost too late. Of course, he at the end says his heart is still green and he will pick up again somewhere else." *Conversations with Frederick Manfred*, ed. John R. Milton (Salt Lake City: University of Utah Press, 1974), pp. 87, 89. I am not convinced that Pier has changed for the better: he has survived, unchanged, too many times in the past. Although the closing scene leaves no doubt in the reader's mind as to what Pier should have learned, there is no clear evidence that Pier himself has learned. He still wonders; he is defiant, even cheerful. I asked Manfred about his comments on Pier, and he ackowledged that Pier hasn't learned very much (it should be noted that John Milton asked him a leading question in *Conversations*). In a letter written after this essay was completed, Manfred clarifies his conception of Pier: "I wanted to show a rather noble fellow named Pier who was asked to come to terms with a 'new place' with a learning that was inadequate. At the end he at least has his vigor left and perhaps in the next phase, next life, such as him will finally have 'learning' enough to handle living in a 'place.' There is a hint that his son has learned. And by learning

I don't mean book learning. I mean life learning. It is supposed to be a tragedy. From the moment you meet him you know he is doomed not to make it in that place" (Manfred to Meldrum, 27 May 1977).

17. Pier tries to reject his father's Old Country ways of farming (p. 9) and Old Country heroic tales (pp. 189–90). But, like Rølvaag's Peder, who finds he is more Norwegian than he ever dreamed, Pier is like his father and repeats the patriarchal pattern.

18. The cleavered house recalls the death of Pier's father, cut in half by a saw that flies away from its mounting (p. 271). Pier's father refuses to adjust to the new machines; ignoring the machine can be fatal, for he should have known not to stand in front of it. Neither Pier nor his father can "think" in the ways demanded by prairie life. Only Pier's son, Teo, reveals that ability to "think"; hope for the future rests with him, but Manfred chooses to focus on Pier's fate, not on Teo's promise.

19. I have alluded to comparisons with Guthrie's *The Big Sky* and Poe's "Fall of the House of Usher," both tragic tales of American literature. Manfred's tale is also a tragedy, but of a very different sort: his hero is even cheerful in the face of disaster, and he expects to begin again, elsewhere. The overall theme is tragic, but the tone is not. Perhaps, however, Manfred's kind of tragedy is even more truly "American" than that of Poe or Guthrie (authors who rely on more traditional tragic modes). Manfred's hero is typically American in thinking he can go someplace else and "make it"; perhaps he will (and American resilience amazes foreigners more than ourselves). But the possibilities of self-fulfillment elsewhere are doubtful, and Pier's lack of insight is in itself tragic: he is another "innocent" American.

20. See Rölvaag, *Their Father's God* (New York: Harper and Brothers, 1931), pp. 330–38.

21. Walter Prescott Webb, "Ended: 400 Year Boom, Reflections on the Age of the Frontier," *Harper's Magazine*, October 1951, pp. 26–33. Webb elaborates his ideas in *The Great Frontier* (Austin: University of Texas Press, 1952).

22. For instance, object relations psychology claims that we are not driven by instincts to defend ourselves from a hostile environment, but are motivated to establish good personal relationships with a loved object (person) as the means of self-fulfillment. Neurosis does not result from frustrations of the pleasure-seeking instinct, but from the continuation of frustrated object-relations in early life which thwart the maturation process. For a discussion of these theories (drawn from the works of Harry Guntrip, D. W. Winnicott, W. R. D. Fairbairn, and others) and how they contrast with Freud's theories, see David Holbrook, " 'Society' and Our 'Instincts': Phantom Authorities for the 'New Moral Revolution,' " *Universities Quarterly* 21 (December 1966): 52–65.

PAUL REIGSTAD

Mythic Aspects of *Giants in the Earth*

RØLVAAG had a remarkable talent for using myth to reinforce the themes of his novels. In *Giants in the Earth*, for example, the protagonist is compared with the *askeladd* of Norwegian folklore, a kind of male Cinderella of notoriously unpromising origins, whose quick wit, imagination, and bravery win him not only fame but even the hand of the king's daughter in marriage. At first the reader of *Giants in the Earth* is permitted to hope that Per Hansa's fortunes will be as favored as those of the *askeladd*. But eventually the hero finds himself at odds with the trolls. In an unusual twist to the conventional happy ending of the folk tales, he is overpowered and destroyed by those powers of darkness. Rølvaag is saying metaphorically that the frontier experience, apparently happy and successful in outcome if only superficially considered, was essentially tragic—costly beyond measure in terms of human suffering and sacrifice.

There are also overtones of the Faust myth in *Giants in the Earth*. I do not wish to suggest that Per Hansa is exactly a Faust figure but rather that he has more in common with the Faustian hero than one might at first suppose. The appeal of the Faust tradition persists because it recognizes certain fundamental moral and philosophical problems: man's desire for power beyond that which is ordinarily human; his complex relationship with good and evil; his sense of the tragedy of human life poised between the possibilities of fulfillment and defeat; and his responsibility for the consequences of his acts. All these problems are as fundamental to *Giants in the Earth* as to the Faust tradition, and Per Hansa, particularly, is forced to face them.

Per Hansa resembles Faust in several respects. Both heroes are creatures of appetite who crave power beyond that which satisfies ordinary men. In Per Hansa's dreams of success on the prairie, he sees himself as ruler of a kingdom vast and wealthy beyond comprehension. In quest of power, both heroes reject the limits imposed by law, custom, and conventional morality. Both display a pride and self-sufficiency which are frightening as well as awe-inspiring to their fellows. At his best Per Hansa is the one person in the settlement of whom it can be said: "We all have a feeling that nothing is ever impossible for you" (p. 445).[1] At his arrogant worst, he must be reminded by his most intimate friend: "You have made [your white-washed house] pretty fine inside, Per Hansa; but He Who is now whitening [with snow] the outside of your walls does fully as well. . . . You shouldn't be vain in your own strength, you know!" (p. 197).

Furthermore, both Faust and Per Hansa encounter an adversary who appears to be—indeed, promises to be—a means of achieving the fulfillment so passionately desired. For Faust it is Mephistopheles; for Per Hansa it is "The Great Plain," lying in brooding silence and, in the words of the novel, "watch[ing] [. . .] breathlessly" (p. 59). Both heroes can be said to accept the challenge of the adversary: Faust by signing with his own blood an agreement with Mephistopheles, Per Hansa by willfully entering the troll kingdom to remove the stakes set by previous settlers on his neighbors' land. Both are men of violent reaction in their determination to transcend limitations, and both are finally defeated by the very limitations they refuse to accept.

By taking a careful look at the mythology of *Giants in the Earth*, it is possible to understand better the processes of cultural growth and adaptation within the context of the middle western prairie, as well as the attendant penalties.

When we call *Giants in the Earth* an antiromantic novel, we mean that Rølvaag has recorded truthfully the whole frontier experience—the terror and suffering and ultimate cost as well as the triumphs.

Part of Rølvaag's genius in working out this theme is reflected in the ambiguity of the title he has chosen, *Giants in the Earth*. At least three explanations of the reference seem possible. Many readers, probably most, are satisfied that the word "giants" is a term of admiration describing Per Hansa and his kind on the great prairies of the Middle West, those brave immigrant settlers whose frontiering spirit led them into alien lands and heroic exploits beyond the endurance of ordinary men. Such was certainly Carl Sandburg's interpretation, for in a review of *Giants in the Earth*, which he called one of the "six most important and fascinating American novels," he described Rølvaag as himself "a giant of the earth," alluding to his firsthand frontier experiences.[2]

But other possibilities are more tempting. Given the elaborate mythological framework of the novel and the presence throughout of the trolls (which are, after all, giants), the adversaries not only of Per Hansa but of all the settlers, it is possible that the "giants in the earth" are the hostile forces threatening frontier civilization—drought, cold, hunger, blizzard, prairie fire, sickness, loneliness, despair. The novel abounds in sinister references to trolls; and the abode of these giants is underground, in Germanic mythology the dwelling place of all evil.

The best explanation, however, is neither of these. It seems most appropriate to assume that the "giants" are indeed the settlers, and to recognize that the term is meant to suggest not only the heroic but also the monstrous in them and to point to their potential for evil.

One must go back to the Genesis account from which Rølvaag takes the epigraph for his novel: "There were giants in the earth in those days; and also after that, when the sons of God came in unto the daughters of men, and they bore children to them, the same became mighty men which were of old, men of renown."[3] These giants appear in the Old Testament account as a sign of increasing wickedness in a civilization ultimately to be destroyed by the great flood. Forgetting their divine origins, these sons of God take to wife the daughters of men. The results of their unions are the giants, half-human, half-divine—monstrous creatures dwelling in the earth. To conceive of Per Hansa and his fellows as "giants" of this order is to find in them not only the godlike but also the gross, ugly, and diabolical.

To Rølvaag the truth about emigration and conquering the frontier included the realization that both enterprises were fraught with spiritual as well as physical danger. Worse than the loneliness and despair of those who could not make the adjustment was the fact that many a soul was deeded to Mammon in exchange for power and riches. Rølvaag has been accused of exaggerating the peril and cost of the landtaking. But as we consider his work from our own perspective in a society concerned about depleted resources, shifting values, cultural poverty, and moral confusion, more and more of us believe that he records an essential part of the total experience.

That the settlers live in the earth in sod huts, like animals or trolls, is proof to Per Hansa's wife, Beret, of the grossness and inhumanity of existence on the prairie. Like the giants of old they too have forgotten their origins, she believes; they have left homes and familiar ways to embrace strange codes and values. To a much greater degree than *Giants in the Earth*, the succeeding novels of Rølvaag's trilogy explore the difficulties of acculturation: the estrangement from much that is familiar and comforting; the loss of the native language and the difficulty of acquiring a new; the pain of separation from loved ones in the homeland; the struggle to found church, school, and state.

The consequences of the settlers' abandoning old loyalties and familiar ways include exploitation of the land, encouraged by the illusion of illimitable horizons and natural resources, and, worse, a growing indifference to the value of human life:

> [People] threw themselves blindly into the Impossible; and accomplished the Unbelievable. If anyone succumbed in the

struggle—and that often happened—another would come and take his place. Youth was in the race; the unknown, the un-tried, the unheard-of, was in the air; people caught it, were intoxicated by it, threw themselves away, and laughed at the cost. Of course it was possible—everything was possible out here. [P. 414]

Giants in the Earth is different from other novels of frontier life because of its fundamental conception of the prairie as the troll-adversary of those who would subjugate it and seize the treasure. Although it is Per Hansa among all the settlers who most ruthlessly sets upon the prairie, and who consequently is most aware of its enmity, all of them experience the dread that something evil is about to happen here:

> It was a singular thing, not a soul in this little colony ever felt wholly at ease, though no one referred to the fact or cared to frame the thought in words. All of a sudden, apparently with-out any cause, a vague, nameless dread would seize hold of them; it would shake them for a while like an attack of nerves; or again, it might fill them with restless apprehension, making them quiet and cautious in everything they did. They seemed to sense an unseen force around them. [P. 61]

When things go wrong, the settlers instinctively blame the enmity of the trolls. They have brought along with them to the New World their primitive fear that to venture into the unknown is to risk straying not into the demon world of hell but into the much more accessible intermediate kingdom of the trolls. In their anxiety to ward off disaster, they band together, though they may be traditionally hostile groups like the Trønders and Helgelanders: "Here they were glad enough to join forces in their common fight against the un-known wilderness. . . . The Great Plain watched them breathlessly" (p. 59).

It is as though the trolls are spying upon the settlers, particularly Per Hansa—the boldest and most insolent of them—eager to pounce upon them at the first misstep, the first intrusion into their kingdom. "This new civilization does not belong here," the Great Silence seems to say. The plundering of the soil is an affront to the trolls. But the settlers cannot be driven away; they can only be harassed, as they are by the locust plague which "proved as certain as the seasons. All that grew above the ground, with the exception of the wild grass, it would pounce upon and destroy; the grass it left untouched because it had grown here ere time was and *without the aid of man's hand*" (p. 340).

Not until Per Hansa commits an act of violence against the trolls does he directly encounter them. Finding the stakes which had been put down the previous autumn on his neighbor's land, he is first stunned, then angered by the malevolence of his adversary: "By God! the trolls must be after him. It was only natural that he should meet them somewhere out here; but to think of their coming in just this dirty fashion! . . . Ah, well, trolls were trolls, no matter how they came! [. . .] Those trolls would not be easy to cope with—not if he knew them!" (pp. 113–14).

For many days Per Hansa struggles with his secret. He recognizes only two choices: to tell the others and then move to new claims, leaving the fruits of their prodigious labors behind them; or to keep his discovery from them and remove the stakes, violating a law as old as mankind itself. Deciding to pull up the stakes, he wastes no time in carrying out his mission. From that moment on till the end of the novel, Per Hansa never recovers the "childlike joyousness" that has been his characteristic response to life: "His face now always wore that forbidding, menacing look, which often would flare up into a flame, and his voice would suddenly be hard as flint. Before his thoughts stood ever the same problem: How would it turn out when the trolls came? Would he be able to hack off their heads and wrest the kingdom from their power? [. . .] For these would be archtrolls, no less" (p. 121).

When he learns that the prior claimants failed to register their claims, Per Hansa triumphantly imagines he will defeat the trolls after all: "He didn't know, just at present, exactly how he was to snatch his neighbours out of the grip of the trolls; but matters would straighten themselves out somehow; the magic sword would be there when he needed it!" (p. 133–34). But having entered the kingdom of the powers of darkness, the domain of the trolls, Per Hansa must pay with his life. The title of the last chapter of the novel prepares us for his fate: "The Great Plain Drinks the Blood of Christian Men and Is Satisfied."

Giants in the Earth is an austere, even grim, vision of life on the frontier. Although it is not without brightness and humor—and an occasional moment of sheer rapture, particularly in Per Hansa's immediate and sensuous response to earth's beauties and pleasures—one cannot escape sharing the dread of impending doom felt by all the characters. The novel has both the stark form and the power of myth, which reduces human experience to the primitive, the elemental. What the reader remembers finally about *Giants in the Earth* is that for the builders, the cost and consequences of establishing a frontier civilization were far greater than we can comfortably remember or imagine; and that the penalties as well as the blessings of their act will be felt by generations still to come.

NOTES

1. O. E. Rölvaag, *Giants in the Earth* (1927; reprint ed., New York: Harper and Row, 1965). Page references in the text are to the Perennial Classics edition. Since Rølvaag frequently uses ellipses as stylistic devices, my omissions are indicated by suspension points enclosed in brackets.

2. Carl Sandburg, review of *Giants in the Earth, Chicago Daily News*, 11 February 1928.

3. Genesis 6:4.

DOROTHY BURTON SKÅRDAL

Life on the Great Plains
in Scandinavian-American Literature

SCANDINAVIAN-AMERICAN LITERATURE came into being in the ethnic newspapers that began to appear around the middle of the nineteenth century and the magazines that came soon after. These periodicals, like many ethnic activities, were often pan-Scandinavian in their early years; but even after Swedes, Norwegians, and Danes had developed their own distinct subcultures in America, the three branches of their literature formed a single whole. Authors differed in their provincial origins, class distinctions, and, above all, in personality. With respect to their experiences as immigrants in the United States, however, these differences fall into patterns determined by time, place, and the interaction of personality with environment rather than by national origin. The literature of all three groups developed at the same time and in the same way, mainly between the 1870s and World War II, and tells the same story about life on the Great Plains.[1]

What today we call ethnicity these immigrant authors called their cultural heritage. Down to the turn of the century many felt no need to define it because they lived its meaning as everything that made them different from other groups in America. They were certainly aware of great diversity in this heritage by class and province of origin—the high culture of the better-educated upper-class minority versus the folk culture of the huge lower-class majority; variation from province to province of dialect, folkways, and custom rooted in centuries of regional isolation; differences between country and city people—but seldom did they realize how drastically the original heritage in these various forms was being modified by industrialization and urbanization progressing at varying speeds in different areas of each country. American students of ethnicity realize they must know as much as possible about the formal culture and intellectual history of the European homelands from which immigrants came, but too often they are not aware that they need knowledge of popular culture and of the history of folk ideas even more. Much illuminating research in ethnology and folklore has been published in Europe in recent years.[2] The more closely we look at regional and provincial variance through time in Scandinavia, the more complex we find patterns of ethnocultural change to be as they crisscross and interact with the transforming forces that also vary by time and place in America. As the end-product of all this permutation, ethnicity in America today is complicated indeed.

Thus, an approach that restricts the study of ethnicity to a single region is likely to be fruitful. By holding place constant, we can see the time variant more clearly; by comparing the reactions of different ethnic groups to the same environment over time, we should understand better the influence of a given area on all kinds of cultural heritages—also American—brought from elsewhere.

A surprising number of Scandinavian-American novels and stories are set in places west of the Missouri River. Norwegian fiction is concentrated primarily in the Dakotas, Swedish and Danish both treat of Nebraska, while only Swedes have written about Kansas. In a number of books the setting is not clearly identified and could be either prairie or plain; Scandinavian writers regularly use the term *praerie* for both. When the characters find abundant trees, however, I assume the author probably means Wisconsin, Iowa, or Minnesota. I have included the Red River Valley, on the border between the Dakotas and Minnesota, mainly because many Norwegian stories are laid in this flat, originally treeless area.

Most typical of all stories about Scandinavians coming to the Great Plains is the characters' initial impression of the vast openness and emptiness of the landscape. This holds for all periods but is most oppressive and frightening to the pioneers. In *Giants in the Earth*, Ole Rølvaag dramatically portrays Beret's fearful reaction to primeval Dakota, where she sees nothing to hide behind; but all kinds of Scandinavian pioneers feel the same dread to some degree because this landscape is so different from any they have known. Above all, it is terrifying to the children, who sense their parents' fear. A Swedish woman writer recalling her childhood years in Kansas entitles her book *I'm Scairt!* and makes fear a central theme: fear of getting lost in the long grass, of the snakes in it, of the Indians who might carry her away, of her mother's homesick tears for Sweden.[3]

Other characters react in different ways to this fear. In the first volume of a trilogy by the Swedish-American Leonard Strömberg, laid in Nebraska,[4] it is a young woman who holds up the courage of all with her strong faith in the future. Her mother is anxious whenever anyone is away because he seems gone to another world, while the wagons of other settlers go on past them and disappear forever, leaving their lonely stretch of plain more desolate that before.

> "But you must remember, Mother, that this is a huge country with space for many people. In time the whole prairie will be settled, and then it won't be so sad here."
> Her mother sighed. It was difficult for her to believe that it would ever be any different out here.[5]

Strömberg's trilogy takes as its subject the transformation of Nebraskan wilderness to modern civilization, which the young heroine foresees and lives through. On the last page of the last novel, she dies full of years and wisdom, after the family farm has been saved for her grown grandsons from the agricultural depression of the 1920s. These young men feel none of their great-grandparents' yearning for Sweden, an important theme of the first novel. As one brother says to the other, "Here is the land of saga, Gunnar, our country and our home."[6] Many other books trace a similar growing acceptance of Great Plains geography by first-generation characters as they become used to it and as the landscape is tamed. Strömberg's novels, like many others, are spangled with lyrical passages describing the beauty of Nebraska nature at all seasons, and some immigrants—unlike Rølvaag's Beret—feel God's closeness as a great blessing on the plains, where his heaven is so near.

All the pioneer novels show Scandinavians acting to change the barren landscape by planting trees as soon as possible. Coming as they have from wooded homelands, their aim is both practical and aesthetic. They need wood and windbreaks and shade from the summer sun, and believe that trees bring more rainfall; but they also need the music of wind in the branches and graceful green for the eye. Some of them raise groves of evergreens with great effort, in times of drought hauling water long distances even more for their saplings than for themselves.

The horrific climate of the Great Plains plays a role in all of this fiction. At least one blizzard is obligatory in every novel, while the opposite extreme of heat in summer is fully as difficult for these people from a northern climate. They are terrified at the crashing thunderstorms and lose their crops to hailstorms with hailstones bigger than they had thought possible. The eternal wind often bothers inland Swedes and Norwegians, while coastal Scandinavians seldom mention it except when a searing blow burns up a year's crop in a few hours. Droughts often bring suspense to a plot by forcing farmers near or into bankruptcy, and floods sometimes cause or solve dramatic problems. Weather is always important to farming people, but Scandinavian-American authors record it as more extreme in this region than elsewhere. They appreciate the much shorter winters, however, and the longer growing season; and although they miss the light nights of the Scandinavian summer, they like the longer winter daylight in this lower latitude. These climatic differences are frequently commented on by characters to each other or mentioned in letters which they write home.

Other natural hazards figure prominently in the literature describing frontier life. Rattlesnakes turn up frequently, clearly a source of dread to people in whose homeland the only poisonous snake is seldom deadly. Every pioneer novel has its plague of grasshoppers, and usually a grass fire scours the plain as well. But the characters have always learned from others how to plow firebreaks and set backfires, so they seldom lose more than outbuildings, haystacks, or a few livestock. Still, poor as they are, these are serious losses in the early years. Such hazards are not described in stories set after the frontier has passed.

Pioneer housing on the Great Plains is more primitive than even the poorest of these immigrants had had back home. Many complain loudly that if they had known how bad things would be on the frontier, they would never have come, but the good characters endure their sod huts or wooden shanties, confident that this is just the beginning, that success of a kind will come if they stay.

> . . . there where a person sank exhausted on his bed of straw and pulled his sheepskin over his face to keep off the rain or snow coming through the leaking roof—there where nothing could be done when the ice-cold wind blew in through the grimy door until one's feet grew stiff, while one roasted from the waist up in immense heat from the little stove stuffed full of straw; there where both the first and the second child was born . . . where one laid the foundation for all the rheumatism which in old age would bow his back and make life a torment; where the only thing that kept one's courage up was to see how the farm and therefore prosperity grew from year to year; there where a man sowed the health of his youth in order to reap freedom from want and the material foundation for his children's future.[7]

Novel after novel describes the drastic changes in living standards as the families "come out of the sod"[8] and build frame houses, then enlarge them or build even finer ones to express their growing prosperity. Many a story records in-

creasing competition in conspicuous consumption (ostentati-
ous turrets and gingerbread decoration on houses, elaborate
furnishings inside), corroborating in detail the observations
of the second-generation Norwegian sociologist Thorstein
Veblen.

Coming to the Great Plains almost exclusively as farmers in search of land, Scandinavian immigrants are shown as
familiar with many farming techniques and able to use their
previous skills in growing small grains and garden vege-
tables. But corn is new to them, and they must seek advice on
every aspect of its cultivation, preferably from Americans.
Some novels give extremely detailed descriptions of the
planting, cultivating, and harvesting of corn, including its
husking and storage in open sheds unlike anything in the Old
Country. American farm machinery is also depicted in exact
particulars at whatever stage of development it had reached
by the time of the story. The authors seem to be accurate here
in the interests of verisimilitude and instruction of Old Country readers in how different such things are in America.

All the characters complain about the American work
tempo and the physical strain of constant overwork. There
are never enough hands to do everything that cries out to be
done, not only in the frontier years, when a single generation
is struggling to build an entire civilization from nothing, but
also throughout the entire period recorded (through the
1920s). An old Dane who comes to spend his last years with
his daughter finds that she

> who home in Denmark had been a lovely, slim girl was now fat,
> stooped, with a grey face and deep wrinkles. . . . As help on the
> big farm, which Hans Nielsen judged needed at least four hired
> men and two girls, his son-in-law had only a teen-age boy.
> Therefore many things were neglected and much was wasted.
>
> The work never ended. There was no pleasant little rest
> period after meals, and the work went on until bedtime.[9]

Newcomers routinely remark on the premature aging, from
overwork in extremes of climate, of those who have gone
before them, in spite of the much better food all enjoy; and
they suffer agonies while learning to keep up. Later, how-

ever, many claim that they first learned what real work is in America. The reader may infer that if they had exerted themselves with equal effort in the Old Country, perhaps they would never have had to emigrate.

Traditional sex roles in work also undergo profound change in America. In the homeland, farm wives were in charge of all barn work except that of caring for the prestigious horse. Women also worked regularly in the fields. During the hectic pioneering period as portrayed in this fiction, women continue to do both barn and field work, taking on even more and harder tasks during the family's difficult early years: "People didn't pay much attention to what was women's work or men's work. The main thing was to get done what lay at hand."[10] After the passing of the frontier, however, a gradual change toward American work patterns appears in the fiction; women are hardly ever pictured at work in the fields and only the older ones continue to do barn work. Rølvaag demonstrates the force of Beret's determination to cling to her Old World ways when in the two sequels to *Giants in the Earth* he shows her still caring for the stock and harvesting corn.[11]

Most of the fiction shows all this toil rewarded. Through the acquisition of free homesteads or cheap land on the Great Plains, most of the Scandinavian farmer characters are able achieve their major goal: improvement of their status and standard of living through ownership of their own farms, which shared in the general rise of land values that followed the development of civilization. For example, a prosperous Dakota farmer, surveying his property one evening, remembers the poverty of his family for generations back in Norway:

> All this: fat horses, great barns, the bulging hayloft—peace, satisfaction based on enough food and sufficient power—this was the way he liked it. . . . And it was all his work and bore the mark of his hands. . . . His chest swelled, his beard bristled, his right hand clenched to a fist. For he remembered a boy who had stood beneath the moon and longed to get ahead. . . . How he burned to get ahead and how he suffered torments because all roads were closed to him. . . . Every way

> he turned, the "better people" stood in his way. . . . Respected
> him no more than a worm in the mud. . . .
>
> He would have liked to point to everything on his beautiful
> farm—at everything that was *his*—and read them a lecture
> . . . small landholder, big landowner, sheriff, bailiff, judge,
> politician, and all the others in Norway who grew fat on the toil
> and simple-heartedness of ordinary folks—they would all have
> fallen to their knees before his wrath.[12]

This quotation has several important aspects. Not only is it
typical of the theme of success in much of this immigrant
literature, but also it shows the deep-felt resentment against
the unjust social system of the home country which motivated
many Scandinavian immigrants to turn their backs on their
cultural heritage and seek to become Americans as rapidly as
possible. No ethnicity for them if they could help it! In addition, it reveals the strong pride in his own achievement of a
self-made man. More pious novels give God credit for a help-
ing hand, and some remember to thank the United States for
its economic opportunities; but Scandinavian characters tend
to take a great deal of credit for their own achievement,
fitting well into the American philosophy of individualism.

In all this fiction, there is little thought for the Indians
whose land the Scandinavians took. Indians of the plains
turn up in pioneer novels only rarely, as a threat or, occasion-
ally, a help to individual settlers, but the possibility that they
have rights which the immigrants are violating is seldom
considered. In a late (1952), unpublished novel, for instance,
a minister tells Norwegian pioneers in the Red River Valley
that a "more innocent self-fulfillment than peopling and cultivating the fertile plains which have lain untouched since
the morning of creation cannot be imagined."[13]

Novels of frontier days on the Great Plains show some
characters giving up the struggle and leaving and others
killed in the battle with the forces of nature, but those who
stick it out and work hard enough end up as the owners of
valuable farms, in justification of the old puritan work ethic,
which is, of course, the Scandinavian peasant work ethic as
well. Stories that carry their characters into the difficult
years of agricultural crises, however, show a darker picture.

For these characters, whose farms have been tied into the market economy of a capitalistic system, it is the economy's ups and downs rather than their own hard work and the weather which will determine their fate. A trilogy by Sophus Winther, the son of Danish immigrants, illustrates the hard fate of those who arrived too late to get cheap land and were condemned to exploitation as rental farmers.[14] This family is forced to buy Nebraska land at peak prices during World War I, and from then on they have no hope of ever escaping the clutches of the mortage company. In the last volume the stalwart old Dane goes down to final defeat as his land is taken and his goods auctioned at forced sale. The bitterness expressed in this trilogy against the unjust American economic system is also to be found in novels by first-generation immigrants.

One such novel—and one which deserves to be better known—is H. A. Foss's *Hvide Slaver* (White Slaves), a Norwegian-American novel of 1892, with much of its improbable plot laid in North Dakota. The book describes the economic enslavement gradually imposed on the agricultural West by eastern and English capitalists from the time of the Civil War down to the time of its publication, in the obvious hope of furthering the Populist cause in the elections of 1892. The author sums up his message in a simile: "It's almost as though all commerce and trade were a cow big enough to stretch from the Atlantic to the Rocky Mountains. The cow is standing with its head in the West, grazing to fill its stomach in the fertile states out here, while its udder is in the East, where others milk it and keep all the milk."[15] Farmers and workers in this novel unite to vote socialism into the American system, and the author obviously hopes the same will happen in real life.

Foss is quite alone in his hope however, for although the Populists, the Farmers' Alliance, and the Non-Partisan League turn up in a few novels, none of the other Scandinavian immigrant authors express support for these movements—let alone socialism.[16] Most of these writers seem to be conservative Republicans who condemn the radicalism of popular movements, portray their leaders as corrupt demagogues, and blame the farmers' economic woes on their own foolishness in borrowing money to buy ever more land and luxuries. American politics are not an important theme in the literature as a whole—surprising, perhaps, since characters in several stories remark that politics and religion are the only interests of their compatriots on the Great Plains above and beyond the daily grind.

In contrast to politics, the immigrant church appears as the central institution of immigrant life in practically every item of fiction. Story after story records graphically many aspects of the Americanization of this institution in spite of its being the only one which American law allowed immigrants to preserve unchanged if they pleased. What the authors perceive to be the pervading piety of their group they show in the frequency of family devotions in most homes, not only before there are any churches but all along. It is very common for these Lutheran immigrants to have brought from the Old Country Bibles, hymnals, and books of sermons following the formal church calendar of the home country. These had been frequently used there in remote areas where church services were scheduled only a few times a year and even then were sometimes canceled by weather. So services led by the family father are a continuation of an Old World practice, like the sacraments of baptism and burial carried out by laymen following the ritual printed in their devotional books. In this, Swedes and Norwegians show that their long tradition of life on separate farmsteads in isolated valleys made them better prepared than immigrants from a village culture (like most Danes) for rural life in the American West.

Practically all the fiction records great controversy within the immigrant churches of the Great Plains, a development which proved to be characteristic of the Scandinavian experience in America. The contending forces of pietism, formalism, and Grundtvigian "happy Christianity," which had managed to coexist within state Lutheran churches in Scandinavia, in the United States exploded in successive schisms within congregations and synods alike.[17] Most authors pay little attention to the theological squabbles behind this uproar, focusing rather on their human causes and effects. Rølvaag gives a superb picture in *Peder Victorious* of Dakota pietists who, shaken by the local tragedy of an unwed mother who murders her baby and kills herself, withdraw from the sinful local church which has accepted all comers to form their own exclusive covenant of the truly righteous. Most of the authors deplore the disastrous effects on the solidarity of the national immigrant group and the local community of this ubiquitous church conflict. A representative novel about a pioneer settlement in Kansas shows the antagonism between formalistic and "separatist" Swedish Lutherans "carried over into the social and economic structure of the community. Stores owned by Lutherans employed clerks of like faith. Separatists did the same. People patronized those of their own creed, and lines were closely drawn. Intermarriage between young people of the two factions was unthinkable."[18]

Even more bitter was the mutual antagonism in many stories between Lutherans on the one hand and "sects" on the other, with Baptists and Methodists appearing most frequently. Small Scandinavian communities frequently acquired far too many different churches for any of them to have decent support. By the turn of the century, however, the heat of all this religious controversy was cooling. A number of Danish-American novels in particular argue for friendship among all kinds of Protestants; one from 1913 reconciles long-estranged Methodist children with their Lutheran mother on her Nebraska deathbed: "I cannot understand that hearts must be sundered because we belong each to our own branch of the Christian church."[19] Evidence of how little these old fights over religion meant to immigrants of this century is seen in the phenomenal popularity of the novels of Leonard Strömberg, a Methodist minister in Nebraska, after World War I. Strömberg keeps the simple piety of his Swedish characters carefully nondenominational, and when his Nebraska pioneers found their local church of indeterminate doctrine, it never suffers a schism. Looking back from a generation later, this author ignores the bitter controversy of the time he is portraying as though it had never happened.

Catholics appear very seldom in Scandinavian immigrant literature of the Great Plains, although virulent anti-Catholicism is present in stories set in older settlements of the Middle West. Rølvaag accords them more space than any other author, dooming to failure, in *Their Fathers' God* (1931), the marriage between a Norwegian Lutheran and an Irish Catholic, as much because of cultural incompatibilities as of religious differences. It is perhaps worth noting that another Norwegian-American novel which began publication as a serial in the same year directly contradicts Rølvaag by picturing *two* Lutheran-Catholic marriages by second-generation characters as happy and successful.[20]

The immigrant literature records another kind of directly ethnic controversy within individual Lutheran churches between those (usually the elderly) who want to keep this institution as Scandinavian as possible, preserving its language, ceremony, and functions in Old World patterns, and those (usually the young) who want it to become like American churches. In a few cases the old win out and their church dies with them, as in a Swedish town in Kansas where the minister had kept everything the way it was back home in Sweden, but the younger generation, not caring about two bells in the church tower but wanting social life and fun to be a part of religion, had gone its own way.[21] Normally, however, the fiction records change in the direction of American church practices, such as the introduction of Sunday schools, graveyards moved from around the church to separate cemeteries, and social events in the church building itself. The long-drawn-out fights in each congregation about the changeover to English appear at various stages: religious instruction for children in both languages at the option of the parents, or regular services in both languages. But then the members go on fighting over which service shall be in the church hall, which in the basement, which at the regular time, which before or after. Gradually, the Scandinavian-language classes and services decline in number and attendance, until they finally end. Then the few old-timers left are bitter indeed: "I can understand a sermon in English as well as I can understand a political talk in the language of this country. But the gospel in English cannot touch the most sensitive strings of my heart, and that was why Gunvor and I sat home and read the Bible verse for the day and sang the old hymns in our mother tongue on Sundays instead of going to church."[22]

Although a considerable number of Scandinavian immigrants on the Great Plains are portrayed as godless in this fiction, joining no church either out of indifference or because they do not believe, most of them come to a bad end, thus testifying to the basic piety of these authors. Piety is probably the most dominant characteristic of the first generation within this ethnic group, at least until the turn of the century. From then on complaints increase about the growing indifference to religion among later immigrants and the second generation, but church membership and regular attendance remain the group norm.

Scandinavian-American authors agree on a number of other group characteristics which they assume or claim to be central to their heritage, not all of which they view with approval. Here the literature is a superb record of immigrants' judgments, attitudes, and feelings about behavioral norms and values within their own group and in the host society.

Fiction about immigrant life on the Great Plains agrees with stories laid elsewhere that alcoholism was the most serious social problem. Prohibition novels are so numerous as almost to make up a separate genre, and drinking or drunkenness appears as a theme in practically all the rest. The collision between the omnipresent American saloon and ancient Scandinavian drinking customs—to imbibe only on rare festive occasions, but then to drink to stupor—proved disastrous, especially on the frontier. Pietists lead the fight against the Demon Rum in this fiction, while high-church leaders are portrayed at first as favoring temperance rather than prohibition. But story after story demonstrates that Scandinavian peasants cannot drink with moderation. The growing puritanism of the group can be traced through the fiction, in which, after the turn of the century, no minister dares be seen with so much as a glass of beer in his hand. There are exceptions to this teetotalism, among whom Rølvaag is the most prominent; but there can be no question about the predominance of the problem of alcoholism.

Materialism is portrayed as the group's besetting sin. Most of the authors picture it as developing in America in response to economic opportunities, not as part of the heritage brought from Europe; but one Norwegian-American sees a clear connection: "It's as though the people were over-eating! They came here, overhungry, and now one chance after another opens before them, and they can't stand it, after being starved so long."[23] The rapid adoption of the American ethos of competition is seen as destroying Old World values of cooperation and mutual support (portrayed as the chief virtue of frontier communities, where all help each other in mutual poverty), and of traditional honor and honesty as well. Characters who preserve the values of their heritage are of course presented as morally superior to those who adopt sharp or dishonest business practices in the spirit of the American drive to get ahead. For instance, a Danish rental farmer in Nebraska follows the Old World ideal of personal honor when hail destroys the mortaged crop on his west eighty. Since the contract had specified that piece of land, he has every legal right to keep the undamaged corn in his other fields; but he decides that would not be honest:

> When I signed that paper, I did it with the full intention of paying . . . wherever I have gone, I have been honest. My word when I was a poor rent farmer was never doubted. In those days before all these written contracts were made, men believed my word as if it were written ten times over in ink. That has been a reward to me many times, when I have had few enough rewards to count. Now I am old and near the grave, shall I sell it for five hundred dollars to a lousy banker? The answer is "No, by God." I'll leave my children a name that bears no stain.[24]

Contrast this with a Danish cattle-raiser in eastern Montana, whose motto is "In business anything goes. If he can cheat his best friend in the sale of a bull, he does so gladly. But if it happens that someone tricks him in a transaction, he bears no grudge. 'I got to keep my eyes open,' he reasons."[25]

The authors agree on several bad effects arising from the

dominant materialism of life on the Great Plains. One is the terrible dullness of their lives: "There's no spiritual or intellectual life here. People have no interests; their thoughts never rise above cattle and pigs and corn."[26] Growing pietism, together with American pressures toward conformity, causes the suppression of much of the folk culture the immigrants had brought along: folk dance and music, ancient festivals, folklore. In some towns ethnic organizations develop to fill this void. A Danish doctor in a South Dakota town, seeking to alleviate the drabness of daily life which has driven four housewives insane within two years, helps found an annual celebration of Danish Constitution Day, a library, and a reading club; but the town also builds a meeting hall and soon has many other societies meeting in it, too: "It was almost impossible to live in Hartland without being a member of three or four organizations."[27] This happens only in strong centers of Scandinavian population; in other settings the complaint of the deadly dullness of ordinary life continues over half a century.

> Very little, if anything, of what we in Smeviken thought was fun seems to interest the fellows here. Do you remember how we used to gather on the mountainside on Sunday afternoons and evenings and amuse ourselves? Do you remember all the stories and folktales we told, and how much fun it was? Do you remember how our songs rang out over field and forest? And all the wrestling matches? And the pranks we played? . . . There is no such life here. No, this is another world, a dead world I was on the point of saying.[28]

And even in centers of ethnic activities, the rituals and celebrations flourish only during the lifetime of the first generation. Newcomers by the time of World War I find most of them dying out and the few that survive often emptied of intellectual and spiritual content in their concentration on social events and insurance.

The dominant materialism is also pictured as harming family life. All the authors agree on home and family as central values in the original Scandinavian heritage. Their peasant emphasis on land ownership as the most important standard of status is based on belief in the intimate relationship between a family and its *seat*. Therefore parents who work themselves almost to death to secure farms for themselves and their children on the Great Plains are bitterly disappointed when the second generation abandons or loses this land and adopts the American pattern of mobility. The immigrant authors see this as rootlessness, and they condemn to moral degradation many a young person who moves to town for a job. Staying on the same land generation after generation is pictured as the highest good, preserving the heart of the European heritage.

The best moral characteristics seen by these authors in the Scandinavian heritage can be summed up as love of the land, strong loyalty within the extended family, thrift and honesty, respect for work, obedience to both civil and religious law, and Protestant piety. The qualities in the American culture that they value most highly are individual freedom, lack of class distinctions, and economic opportunity— all adding up to the chance for each person to develop as he or she chooses: the American dream. That dream is often limited or denied by circumstances, but the stories show the chances for individual fulfillment and social betterment to be much better in the United States than in the homelands for people of lower-class origin at least during the time of this literature. However, the fiction records the authors' recognition that Scandinavian immigrants paid a high price for social betterment on the Great Plains, in the physical strain of overwork, the loss of many values, and the psychological strain of being strangers in a foreign country.

Homesickness is a universal theme in this literature, measuring the unexpected pain of hearts divided by partial socialization in two cultures. Most Scandinavian immigrants who settled on the Great Plains had come from stable peasant communities with ancient roots, and many suffered from the loss of cultural and family ties broken by their emigration. Rølvaag's Beret is the classic symbol of this problem. She expresses its most extreme form, but homesickness is the most prominent and typical feeling expressed throughout all periods and in all settings covered by Scandinavian-Ameri-

can literature. It is especially strong in the poetry. The best
Swedish-American poet, Arthur Landfors, expressed a common group experience in the following poem:

> There stands an ancient house somewhere,
> which was my home.
> No matter where I go, it will
> remain my home.
>
> My father's father fashioned it
> and ate his bread
> beside its fire, and through its gate
> was borne when dead.
>
> Above the threshold of the door
> my father too,
> when death had closed his weary eyes,
> was carried through.
>
> A century's peace deposited
> its hallowed load
> in grandfather's and father's and
> the clan's abode.
>
> I'll not be carried out when dead
> from that gateway,
> but still I claim and cherish well
> the right to say
>
> that though I never find firm ground
> to place my foot,
> still somewhere, somewhere far away
> my heart has root.[29]

Christmas is a special Scandinavian family and community
festival, and the steady stream of poems of homesickness in
the immigrant community swelled to a veritable flood each
year at Christmastime. These lines by a leading Danish-
American poet, August Bang, are typical:

Now all the bells are chiming from Denmark's snow-white churches,
and all the shining parish is tuned to holy joy.
      . . . But I, alas, poor dreamer,
who sit here in Dakota and dream again of yore,
I seem to feel the light of Christmas love shine round me,
and hear my mother beg, "Come home once more!"[30]

Certainly not all immigrants were equally afflicted by home-sickness, however. Rølvaag's Per Hansa is the opposite of his wife, Beret; he is the strong and buoyant pioneer facing the challenge of the unknown with joyful hope. Both types are present throughout Scandinavian-American literature from its beginning in the 1870s, as are all possible variations of character between these extremes.

What can we conclude about Scandinavian ethnicity on the Great Plains from a survey of this fiction? First, the fiction reveals no significant differences between the life of this immigrant group and the lives of similar groups which settled in other parts of the Middle West. From the Rockies on the west to Illinois on the east, Scandinavian immigrant experience is recorded as a unified whole, except for the scarcity of large cities beyond the Missouri. Omaha and Lincoln are the only cities mentioned in stories set on the Great Plains, and they are no more than mentioned. There is no description of anything like the rich ethnic activity recorded in stories set in Chicago and Minneapolis. Therefore, the businessmen and workers who populate the city novels do not appear: rather, the characterizations are only of rural and small-town people, and these reveal no differences from the country folk and townspeople of the prairies to the east.

Second, although this literature displays consistent agreement in the record of what might be called the *typical* facts of the entire range of immigrant life—from the physical level of landscape, housing, tools, and work techniques, through the development of institutions like politics and churches and schools, to the behavioral patterns of family and social life, and values on the highest levels of abstraction—still there is great variation in what the authors emphasize and how they interpret what they record. Certainly, the environment to which the immigrants came varied greatly according to time of arrival; and there were differences as well among the immigrants themselves, who came from a variety of regions during particular periods of time. But the chief cause of the variation in these accounts—and the decisively complicating factor in the effort to use literature as historical source material—lies with the individual-

ity of each writer, with, that is, the personality of the recorder, which determines so much of what he sees.

The next step in the development of techniques for using
literature as source material for history therefore must be the
detailed study of individual authors. Only when we know
what kind of people they were can we evaluate accurately the
reliability of their evidence. We must account for the widely
different ways in which they view the life of the group they
describe. The differences among them are amazing, and explain in large measure why they wrote from such varying
points of view.[31]

Ethnic literature is of great value in the study of ethnicity. Its central theme is change. It records in infinite detail
how the immigrant heritage was modified by American influences on everyday experience into the ethnicity of today,
which continues to change—now, it seems, by seeking re-
newal from its original sources.

NOTES

1. For a survey of Scandinavian immigrant literature, see my
book *The Divided Heart: Scandinavian Immigrant Experience
through Literary Sources* (Lincoln: University of Nebraska Press,
1974), pp. 27–52. My article "Danish-American Literature: A Call to
Action," *Scandinavian Studies* 48 (Autumn 1976): 405–25, gives
additional information about the Danish branch of the literature,
while "Scandinavian-American Literature: A Frontier for
Research," *Swedish Pioneer Historical Quarterly* 28 (October 1977):
237–51, focuses on the Swedish branch. For a recent survey of
Norwegian-American literature, see Gerald Thorson, "Pressed
Flowers and Still-Running Brooks: Norwegian-American Literature," in *Proceedings: Comparative Literature Symposium,* Texas
Technological University, vol. 9, pt. 2 (Lubbock, Texas, 1979), pp.
375–94.

2. For a survey of research in this field in Norway, see Ronald
Gambo, "Folkloristic Research in Norway 1945–1976," *Norveg
Folkelivsgransking* 20 (1977): 221–86.

3. Anna Olsson, *I'm Scairt! Childhood Days on the Prairie*
(Rock Island, Ill.: Augustana Book Concern, 1927). This work has
been retranslated from the 1917 Swedish original by Martha Win-

blad as *A Child of the Prairie,* ed. Elizabeth Jaderborg (Lindsborg, Kansas: privately printed, 1978).

4. Leonard Strömberg's trilogy has been published in four volumes by De Unges Forlag in Oslo: *Der praerien blomstrer* [Where the prairie blooms] (4th ed., 1969); *Familien på Holmebo* [The family at Holmebo] (1965); *Hemmeligheten på Holmebo* [The secret at Holmebo] (1965); and *Storm over viddene* [Storm over the plains] (2nd ed., 1956). These novels were published earlier in Sweden, the first in 1933.

5. Strömberg, *Der praerien blomstrer,* p. 40. My translation here and in all citations to follow where the title is not in English.

6. Strömberg, *Storm over viddene,* p. 244.

7. Kristofer Janson, *Praeriens saga: Fortaellinger fra Amerika* [The saga of the prairie: stories from America] (Chicago: Skandinavens Bogtrykkeri, 1885), p. 7.

8. Simon Johnson uses this phrase in an unpublished manuscript novel, "Stier på ny jord" [Paths on new earth] (1952), p. 90.

9. Carl Hansen, *Landsmaend* [Compatriots] (Cedar Falls, Iowa: Dansk Boghandel, 1908), p. 53.

10. Kristian Ostergaard, *Danby Folk* (Cedar Falls, Iowa: Dansk Boghandel, 1925), p. 11.

11. O. E. Rölvaag, *Peder Victorious* (New York: Harper & Brothers, 1929) and *Their Fathers' God* (New York: Harper & Brothers, 1931).

12. Simon Johnson, *Fallitten paa Braastad* [The bankruptcy at Braastad] (Minneapolis: Augsburg Publishing House, 1922), pp. 8–10.

13. Johnson, "Stier på ny jord," p. 109.

14. Sophus Keith Winther, *Take All to Nebraska* (1936; reprint ed., Lincoln: University of Nebraska Press, 1975); *Mortgage Your Heart* (1937; reprint ed., New York: Arno Press, 1979); and *This Passion Never Dies* (New York: Macmillan, 1938).

15. H. A. Foss, *Hvide slaver: En social-politisk skildring* (Christiania: P. Omtvedts Forlag, 1893), p. 207. For a full analysis of this book and comparison of it to historical sources, see Svein Ove Sandvik, "H. A. Foss, Norwegian-American Author and Editor" (M.A. thesis, University of Oslo, 1977), pp. 58–71.

16. For the interesting story of a fiery radical who was an outstanding exception (but who did not belong to the Great Plains), see Odd Gunnar Andreassen, "Lars Andreas Stenholt, Norwegian-American Author" (M.A. thesis, University of Oslo, 1977).

17. Bishop N. F. S. Grundtvig (1783–1872) founded a movement within the Danish state church that emphasized the history, art, and folk traditions of the nation as an essential part of its religious heritage. Emphasizing joy in the life of this world, the Grundtvigian movement came to be called "happy Christianity." It had profound influence on the development of national romanticism

in nineteenth-century Scandinavia, which in turn helped mold the ideas of many Scandinavian-American authors, not least Rølvaag. See Gudrun Hovde Gvåle, *O. E. Rølvaag, nordmann og amerikaner* (Oslo: Universitetsforlaget, 1962), part I.

18. Anna M. Carlson, *The Heritage of the Bluestem* (Kansas City, Mo.: Burton Publishing Co., 1930), p. 44.

19. Kristian Ostergaard, *Dalboerne* (Copenhagen: Nationale Forfatteres Forlag, 1913), p. 199.

20. Einar Lund, *Solveig Murphy,* novel serialized in *Ved Arnen* 58—literary supplement of *Decorah-Posten*—from no. 20 (1 December 1931) to no. 29 (2 February 1932).

21. Gustaf Malm, *Harute: Verklighetsbild ur svenskamerikanarnes hvardagslif* [Out here: true pictures from Swedish-American everyday life] (Lindsborg, Kans.: author's publication, ca. 1919), pp. 107–8.

22. H. A. Foss, *Valborg* (Oslo: P. Omtvedts Forlag, 1928), p. 147.

23. Simon Johnson, *From Fjord to Prairie* (Minneapolis: Augsburg Publishing House, 1916), pp. 295–96.

24. Winther, *This Passion Never Dies,* pp. 180–81.

25. M. Sorensen, *Traekfugle: Skitser af danskes liv i Amerika* [Birds of passage: sketches of Danes' life in America] (Odense: Milo, 1903), pp. 16–17.

26. M. Sorensen, *Hinsides Atlanten* [Beyond the Atlantic] (Copenhagen: T. R. Tomassen, 1906), p. 72.

27. Carl Hansen, *Praeriefolk* (Copenhagen: Hagerup, 1907), p. 125.

28. O. E. Rølvaag, *The Third Life of Per Smevik* (Minneapolis: Dillon Press, 1971), p. 53. This work was originally published as *Amerika-Breve, fra P. A. Smevik til hans far og bror i Norge* [Letters from America, from P. S. Smevik to his father and brother in Norway] (Minneapolis: Augsburg Publishing House, 1912).

29. Arthur Landfors, *Träd som bara grönska* [Trees that grow only leaves] (Stockholm: FIB:s Lyrikklubb, 1962), poem, "Hemmet," p. 16–17. My translation.

30. August L. Bang, *Livet i vold* [In the throes of life] (Cedar Falls, Iowa: Dansk Boghandel, 1938), pp. 135–36. My translation.

31. I have initiated a research project at the University of Oslo in which graduate students write the equivalent of master's theses on Norwegian-American writers. One by one these almost forgotten minor figures are coming into focus. In addition to the theses noted above by Sandvik and Andreassen, (notes 15 and 16), the following have been completed: Hilda Petra Brungot, "Dorthea Dahl, Norwegian-American Author of Everyday Experience" (1977); Baard Meyer-Myklestad, "Einar Lund, Norwegian-American Journalist and Author" (1977); Jan-Eirik Imbsen, "Johannes B. Wist, Norwegian-American Leader" (1977); Liv Smith, "Ole Amundsen Buslett,

Norwegian-American Author" (1978); Barbara Ann Alnaes, "Borghild M. Dahl, Second Generation Norwegian-American Author" (1978); Veslemoy Steensnaes, "Nicolai Severin Hassel, The First Norwegian-American Novelist" (1978); Ole Podhorny, "Christian Nephi Anderson, Popular 'Mormon' Author of Norwegian Origin" (1980); and Sissel Marie Gulmoen, "Immigrant Experience and the West as Depicted in the Works of the Norwegian-American Author Olai Aslaggson" (1980).

BERNICE SLOTE

Willa Cather and Plains Culture

THE GREAT ROUND of plains and sky which enveloped Willa Cather as a child of nine, coming to northern Webster County, Nebraska, from Virginia with her family in 1883, was not, she thought, a place for any ordinary kind of life. Thirty years later in a 1913 interview she recalled the landscape as wild and bleak; she had felt "thrown out into a country as bare as a piece of sheet iron," where only faint trails were marked over the bunch grass, and no fences traced the land. There were no patterns, only space: "it was a kind of erasure of personality."[1] She was right: life for her in early Nebraska was not ordinary but extraordinary; she had come at one of those turns of history when individual experience is intensified into rebirth. Soon, of course, she found that the unmarked plains were not the end of everything, but the beginning of freedom, growth, fecundity. The beginning of a history.

In Willa Cather's novels, especially those of the decade 1913 to 1923 *(O Pioneers!, The Song of the Lark, My Ántonia, One of Ours, A Lost Lady)*, the physical sense of the plains—grasses and trees, blizzards and drought, high skies and sunsets, all the changing seasons—is immediate, rich, and real. But this sense of the physical world is not something which came to her only in recollection; even her earliest stories in the 1890s gave a sense of passionate identity with the country and the land. The condemned man in "The Clemency of the Court" (1893)[2] had always loved the plains, "ever since he was a little fellow, when the brown grass was up to his shoulders and the straw stacks were the golden mountains of fairyland" (p. 520). Though he is called Russian, Serge had been born "in the western part of the state." In prison he thinks "how lovely the plains would look in the morning when the sun was up; how the sunflowers would shake themselves in the wind, how the corn leaves would shine and how the cobwebs would sparkle all over the grass" (pp. 521–22). Cather wrote more ominously of "the yellow scorch" of the drought (p. 495) and the stinging snow in "On the Divide" (1896), but the general tone of her feeling about the plains was that of "Tommy, the Unsentimental" (1896), a story of a girl who belongs to the plains, good or bad. Tommy comes back from school in the East homesick for the intense blue of the sky. "And this wind," she says, "this hateful, dear, old everlasting wind that comes down like the sweep of cavalry and is never tamed or broken. . . . I used to get hungry for this wind! I couldn't sleep in that lifeless stillness down there" (p. 476). In the Introduction to *My Ántonia* Willa Cather places us deeply in that land of "burning summers when the world lies green and billowy beneath a brilliant sky, when one is fairly stifled in vegetation, in the colour and smell of strong weeds and heavy harvests; blustery winters with little snow when the whole country is stripped bare and grey as sheet-iron."[3]

With the term "sheet-iron" we are thrown back to her earliest memory of the unresponsive, uncultivated land when she arrived ("a country as bare as a piece of sheet iron"). But what had happened between 1883 and the publication of *My Ántonia* in 1918 is that she had come to see the time of her youth, the time of settlement, as a burgeoning of life, a movement in history. Willa Cather does not write of the plains outside that sense of motion in time, the human changes that interlock with the plains. When she was sixteen, graduating from Red Cloud High School, she opened her oration with this statement: "All human history is a record of

an emigration, an exodus from barbarism to civilization."
The idea of man's pilgrimage through time was strong in her
(partly from reading, of course); it relates to all the ancestral
myths of home-seeking, to biblical and medieval wanderings
over deserts to promised lands and sacred shrines; it relates
to human settlement and human productivity on the wild
land of the plains. In *My Ántonia* she wrote: "The windy
springs and the blazing summers, one after another, had
enriched and mellowed that flat tableland; all the human
effort that had gone into it was coming back in long, sweeping
lines of fertility. The changes seemed beautiful and harmonious to me; it was like watching the growth of a great man or of
a great idea" (p. 306).

In its own form and arrangement *My Ántonia* parallels
the movement of history and the settlement of the plains. The
first section is all of the land, mostly unsettled except for a few
families; we are made aware of animal life close to the soil
(prairie dogs, snakes, rabbits); we are strongly conscious of
the great primeval sea of red grass, the brilliant autumn sun.
Houses are for shelter: "Our lives centred around warmth
and food and the return of the men at nightfall" (p. 66).
Simple but deep relationships are between individuals or
families. The next section moves to the town of Black Hawk, a
cluster of flimsy houses, a place of businesses and group
interchange; we are not on the land but on streets; higher,
trees and birds rise over the river. Houses often confine for "a
guarded mode of existence" (p. 219) (movement is out, not in).
There are complex social relationships and class distinctions.
From the small town we are taken to the city and move
outward to the university, the expansion of learning, imagination, the arts. The narrator, Jim Burden, goes to a farther
world, out of our view. His return is to a place and people
altered by time, by gains and by losses—yet some of it still a
part of himself.

The change through growth is illustrated in two strik-
ingly parallel passages in *My Ántonia,* one when Jim is sitting alone in a sunny hollow of his grandmother's garden,
sheltered by grasses, and a later one when he is with Ántonia
in a clearing like a cup of sun, sheltered by the trees of the

orchard she had planted and cared for. In Jim's first happy encounter with the earth he leans against a pumpkin, sees only the sky above him, notes "ground-cherry bushes growing along the furrows" in their "papery triangular sheaths." There are grasshoppers, gophers, and red bugs that move "in slow squadrons" around him. In this close union with the earth, Jim is "entirely happy" (p. 18). In the later passage all of the earth-growing details are supplanted by larger, taller ones. Jim and Ántonia (with children near them) are seated in a grape arbor in the middle of an apple orchard which is sheltered by hedges of locust and mulberry. They could "see nothing but the blue sky above them. . . . The afternoon sun poured down on us through the drying grape leaves. The orchard seemed full of sun, like a cup, and we could smell the ripe apples on the trees." The crabapples are described with the same delicate exactness used for the ground-cherries earlier. The military bugs are replaced by ducks that, Ántonia said, "always reminded her of soldiers" (pp. 341–42). These two moments of the epiphany of sun and earth, early and late in the book, mirror each other like a grown person and the child he was.

The real West to Willa Cather was the West of settlement, of the immigration of peoples from many parts of the world—people she often saw as exiles (even as she once felt the separation from a homeland). To many readers, this gathering of a population drawn from the Old World is a watermark of Willa Cather's subject matter, and indeed it seemed to her a mark of Nebraska as she wrote about the state in an article first published in the *Nation* in 1923: "Colonies of European people, Slavonic, Germanic, Scandinavian, Latin, spread across our bronze prairies like the daubs of color on a painter's palette. They brought with them something that this neutral new world needed even more than the immigrants needed land."[4]

In 1897, when she first heard the largo from Dvořák's symphony "From the New World," she found her own country in the music:

> . . . before you stretch the empty, hungry plains of the Middle West. Limitless prairies, full of the peasantry of all the nations

of Europe; Germans, Swedes, Norwegians, Danes, Huns, Bohemians, Romanians, Bulgarians, Russians and Poles, and it seems as though from each of those far scattered lights that at night mark the dwellings of these people on the plains, there comes the song of a homesick heart.[5]

The theme of homesickness and exile is also in some of her early stories, those published by 1900: the Bohemian in "Peter" (1892) who commits suicide, the mad Dane in "Lou, the Prophet" (1892), the condemned Russian Serge in "The Clemency of the Court" (1893), the lonely giant Canute Canuteson in "On the Divide" (1896), and even a Virginia couple in the West in the delicately sophisticated story "The Sentimentality of William Tavener" (1900). But other stories, like "Eric Hermannson's Soul" (1900), invoke strongly the better future that was always in the Western dream. At the end of Dvořák's largo movement, Willa Cather wrote, "there comes that long, high final note on the wind instruments that seems to rise out of that vortex of sound like an aspiration, seems to rise clear into the evening sky and tremble there like a star. It is like the flight of the dove over the waste of waters, that last note, there is all the hope of the new world in it."

Willa Cather drew her material from her own early experiences in Webster County. Her cast of characters from many lands—particularly the Swedes, Danes, Norwegians, Bohemians, French, and Russians (in *O Pioneers!* and *My Ántonia* especially)—have substance in the actual population of the sections of Webster and Franklin counties near the Cather homestead. The 1885 census lists in that vicinity immigrants from Sweden, Norway, Denmark, Moravia, Prussia, the German areas of Russia, and French Canada. The French settlement of LaPorteville was the prototype for the village of Sainte-Agnes in *O Pioneers!*. It was an unusual concentration of nationalities.

Willa Cather's sympathetic use of the varying cultures of these immigrant peoples is more remarkable when viewed in the context of Hamlin Garland's generally harsh treatment of them in his stories of the 1890s, and, for example, a passage from an almost unknown (and perhaps the first) novel of

Nebraska, the 1891 *John Auburntop, Novelist,* by Anson
Uriel Hancock. In the book, an old pioneer in the eastern part
of the state, near Seward, is asked by university student John
Auburntop about some Bohemians he had met earlier in his
travels. Yes, says the pioneer,

> "them Bohemians is taking the kintry. Formerly, we was all
> Amerikins in this neighborhood; naow about half of us is gone
> and every time one of us goes a furriner steps in. They'll take
> the kintry. There's a hull Swede settlement I know on, where
> the 'arly settlers was all Yankees. They have their *kirche,* they
> call it, and take Dutch newspapers and talk Dutch, an' you'd
> think if you got among 'em you was surely in their own kintry
> and not in Ameriky. . . . But I s'pose it'll be different a hundred
> year from now; we'll all be Amerikins then."[6]

Some were American, and some were foreigners; and that
made all the difference.

Willa Cather caught that dissonance truthfully in *My
Ántonia.* The Scandinavian or Bohemian "hired girls" from
the country who worked in Black Hawk to help their families
may have been more joyously alive than some of the constrained small-town people, but Black Hawk boys were to
marry respectability in Black Hawk girls: "The country girls
were considered a menace to the social order. Their beauty
shone out too boldly against a conventional background" (p.
201). These girls were not uneducated: they had learned from
poverty, from their parents. They had been "early awakened
and made observant by coming at a tender age from an old
country to a new" (p. 198). This kind of understanding, placed
in the richness of Cather's fictional mode, and its special
evocation in *My Ántonia,* was what caused Rose Rosicky to
write in her 1929 book, *A History of Czechs in Nebraska,* an
inscription: "To Willa S. Cather / who gave Bohemian /
immigrants of Nebraska / a permanent place / in American
literature."

Willa Cather's use of non-European ethnic groups such
as blacks or plains Indians is minimal in her early stories.
She lived in Nebraska in the 1880s and 1890s, when Indians
were noticed in the newspapers chiefly as warring tribes with
dirty living habits. In any case, they were far from Red Cloud,

and Wounded Knee was only a column or so of print. Literary views in Nebraska were composed in highly romanticized legends, some in Hiawathan style, like E. E. Blackman's *Niobrara's Love Story* (1900). There was a Negro community in Lincoln, often favorably reported in the press, but the most memorable contact would be a concert by Blind Boone or Blind Tom. Such a musician has an important place in *My Ántonia* in the episode of Blind d'Arnault, who gives a concert in Black Hawk and plays at the hotel later, where his intense and sensuous music gives Ántonia her first release of freedom in dance.

By the time she wrote *My Ántonia,* however, Willa Cather had been deeply moved by the Indians she began to know in 1912 when she stayed for several months in the Southwest. Her novels, in contrast to her early short stories, make extensive use of what she observed of Indian qualities and experience. This ancient world of the Southwest, which extended history for her, became central to her 1915 novel *The Song of the Lark* (in which she also used Mexicans, though primarily as symbols for a music-loving, free, artistic temperament), *The Professor's House* (1925), and, of course, *Death Comes for the Archbishop* (1927). In other books she touches on Indians ways. *My Ántonia,* for example, has a subtle image for the imagination. In the first light snow Jim Burden sees on a slope "faintly marked in the grass, a great circle where the Indians used to ride. . . . Whenever one looked at this slope against the setting sun, the circle showed like a pattern in the grass; and this morning, when the first light spray lay over it, it came out with a wonderful distinctness, like strokes of Chinese white on canvas. The old figure stirred me as it had never done before and seemed a good omen for the winter" (p. 62). Some thought prisoners had been tied to a stake in the center of the circle and tortured; others, less melodramatically, that horses had been trained there. Some people were seen in likeness: "[Mrs. Gardener] was tall, dark, severe, with something Indian-like in the rigid immobility of her face" (p. 182). And at the old Burden homestead was a pioneer, Widow Steavens: "She was brown as an Indian woman, tall, and very strong" (p. 307).

The heritage of many cultures gained and blended through immigration to the Great Plains was primary in Willa Cather's subject matter. Perhaps nowhere else can we get the extended detail, the variety, the clear perception of this mosaic that we find in her writing, both early and late.

To her the settlers from the Old World may have been exiles, yet they were also figures in that long chain of effort that has led man (in her terms) from barbarism to civilization. They were uprooted people (even as she and her family had been changed), sometimes unequal to the land, sometimes stronger than misfortune. They came for land, for money, for duty, for love, or, like the "American" villain of *My Ántonia*, Wick Cutter, to have their way. "In every frontier settlement there are men who have come there to escape restraint" (p. 209). It is only fair to say that in the same book she has a Bohemian villain, too—Peter Krajiek, who had cheated and deceived his own countrymen, the Shimerdas: "Krajiek was their only interpreter, and could tell them anything he chose" (p. 20). And there were conflicts between national groups, just as there were between "Americans" and "foreigners": "Bohemians has a natural distrust of Austrians," says one of the hired men in *My Ántonia* (p. 21). When asked to explain, he simply lays it on politics, something too long (and, we know, too long ago) to explain. Bohemian Ántonia, too, has a warning to Jim Burden: "You won't go and get mixed up with the Swedes, will you?" (p. 224).

Although the exiles had most often come for land, they were often not suited for the battle. John Bergson, in *O Pioneers!*, "had the Old-World belief that land, in itself, is desirable," but "no one understood how to farm it properly" (pp. 21–22). Bergson's neighbors knew even less than he; they had not worked on farms before but had been handworkers—tailors, locksmiths, joiners, cigar-makers. Bergson came from work in a shipyard; Mr. Shimerda (in *My Ántonia*) had been a weaver; Peter Sadelack (in the story "Peter") had been a violinist in a theater orchestra in Prague; Anton Rosicky (in "Neighbour Rosicky" [1930]) had been a tailor. Lena Lingard's grandfather, like others, she says in *My Ántonia*, had been a man with a high position in the Old Country—"but that's all the good it does us!" (p. 242).

We are always aware of the stern effect of the new land on its people. The weaver Shimerda and the violinist Sadelack committed suicide (both fictional events based upon a real happening in Webster County in 1881). Other effects were less violent, but real. For a time, Ántonia must work and dress like a man. When they first came, Ántonia and her sister were famished for fruit, and they would "wander for miles along the edge of the cornfields, hunting for ground-cherries" (p. 31). Also in *My Ántonia,* Anna Hansen's Norwegian grandmother "craves fish all the time" (p. 239). Some, like Mrs. Bergson in *O Pioneers!*, never wanted to come to America but adapted all the same. With Mrs. Bergson it was an intent battle with time and the country:

> Alexandra often said that if her mother were cast upon a desert island, she would thank God for her deliverance, make a garden, and find something to preserve. Preserving was almost a mania with Mrs. Bergson. Stout as she was, she roamed the scrubby banks of Norway Creek looking for fox grapes and goose plums, like a wild creature in search of prey. She made yellow jam of the insipid ground-cherries that grew on the prairie, flavoring it with lemon peel; and she made a sticky dark conserve of garden tomatoes. She had experimented even with the rank buffalo-pea, and she could not see a fine bronze cluster of them without shaking her head and murmuring, "What a pity!" When there was nothing more to preserve, she began to pickle. [P. 29]

She did not compromise with the plains. She endured but she did not love. It is her daughter Alexandra who represents all those who loved the land better than to make a new history of jealousy and wars, Alexandra, who placed her heart in the long grass, with insects and birds and the sun: "Under the long shaggy ridges, she felt the future stirring" (p. 71). For the immigrant and the raw land, it was a pattern of dark and light.

In many ways we are reminded in the Cather books of ties between the Old World and the New—links of memory, habit, or desire. The Shimerdas (in *My Ántonia*) brought along dried mushrooms from the forests of Bohemia. An insect reminds Ántonia of an old beggar woman's songs. In his saloon Anton Jelinek "kept rye bread on hand and smoked fish and strong imported cheeses to please the foreign palate" (p. 217). The elder blossoms by the river make Ántonia homesick: "We have this flower very much at home, in the old country. It always grew in our yard and my papa had a green bench and a table under the bushes" (pp. 235–36). There had been "beautiful talk" in the old country, talk of music, of woods, of God, and of when they were young. Tiny Soderball says, "It seems like my mother ain't been so homesick, ever since father's raised rye for her" (p. 239). They do the polka, a schottische, and Bohemian dances in "The Bohemian Girl" (1912); there are folk songs of the north—music like Grieg's—in "Eric Hermannson's Soul." Neighbour Rosicky reads a Bohemian newspaper printed in Omaha. In *My Ántonia*, the Burdens' hired man, Otto, has Christmas decorations of "brilliantly coloured paper figures" from Austria (p. 83). And even Jim Burden, an immigrant from Virginia, has brought along a collection of "Sunday-School cards and advertising cards" from his "old country" (p. 81).

The mingling of old and new on the actual frontier plains was pervasive. Thanksgiving dinner at Lincoln's Windsor Hotel in 1895 featured—among many items—saddle of venison, opossum with browned sweet potatoes, prairie chicken pie, and broiled quail on toast, but also raw oysters, shrimp salad, English plum pudding, and California grapes. Oysters (shipped in frozen, in cakes of ice) were a sign of civilization in the young cities. The elegant and exotic countered the mud, wind, and sunflowers. Even in Red Cloud, Willa Cather in 1896 sent to Chicago for fresh strawberries to serve at a wedding breakfast she prepared. The great world flowed in. Merchants from small towns and cities traveled to Europe and returned with pianos, oriental rugs, fine china. Richard Mansfield and many other important actors and actresses came to Nebraska; Willa Cather knew them. She saw and reviewed scores of plays and musical performances. From childhood she knew the Bible and such English classics as

Shakespeare and *Pilgrim's Progress*. But as early as high school she also read Russian novels and translated the *Aeneid*. In the 1890s she went to the twenty-year-old University of Nebraska, where they taught Sanskrit—and modern authors like Browning. For Willa Cather life on the plains was genuinely international, in time as well as in geography. Demonstrably, it was history in process, in concentration.

The larger world is always there in the Cather fiction. Alexandra Bergson once says to her friend Carl Linstrum, "If the world were no wider than my cornfields, if there were not something beside this, I wouldn't feel that it was much worth while to work" (p. 124). That other life of the plains Willa Cather recreates in characters like Dr. Archie, the music teacher Wunsch, and Thea Kronborg with her yearning for life and art, in the first sections of *The Song of the Lark*; the Rosens, whose home is both library and refuge for Vickie Templeton in "Old Mrs. Harris"; the Harlings in *My Ántonia*, who teach Ántonia manners and housekeeping skills. It was important to many people in Willa Cather's pioneer world (both real and fictional) to demonstrate that they had not left civilization. I have heard of one Nebraska lady who, when she did not have ice to serve her guests, would fill an opaque pitcher with cold water directly from the well and put in a handful of buttons to simulate the sound of tinkling ice.[7] Marian Forrester, in *A Lost Lady* (1923), is one who upholds civilized behavior, though she is much more—an entrancing and enigmatic woman who gives life to those who love her. Mrs. Forrester represents one facet of that wider world of Alexandra's. Thea Kronborg finds it, too, in music. Thea's life on the plains is inextricably joined with art. When she hears in Chicago the largo from Dvořák's *New World* Symphony (even as Willa Cather herself had been moved by it), Thea finds in the music "the sand hills, the grasshoppers and locusts, all the things that wakened and chirped in the early morning; the reaching and reaching of high plains, the immeasurable yearning of all flat lands. There was home in it, too; first memories, first mornings long ago; the amazement of a new soul in a new world" (p. 251). The world was wider than the cornfields, but the cornfields stayed in it.

Willa Cather also records the recession of some of the high values of the rising years on the plains. There is a turn downward. Alexandra's brothers grow up to be quarrelsome about money, politics, position; Ivy Peters (in *A Lost Lady*) destroys the wild and delicate beauty of the Forrester marsh; the cutting down of an orchard begins in *Lucy Gayheart* (1935). Still, the checkerboard fields of alternating dark and light that marked the plains of Nebraska in such a brief time are there to demonstrate the beauty of order and productivity.

Willa Cather did not write her fiction to record the culture of the plains, though it is there in stunning physical detail. She *used* it, not for history but for individual trails of the imagination. She wrote in her 1922 essay, "The Novel Démeublé": "Whatever is felt upon the page without being specifically named there—that, one might say, is created."[8] From the page can come images, perceptions, lives, but it is the sense we have about them, our emotional response to the meanings we feel rather than understand, that will most completely fit Cather's intention. For example, recall in *My Ántonia* the picnic of the hired girls and Jim Burden by the river and on a bluff nearby. Though they are fixed in one spot of the plains, memory, mystery, imagination, and ancestral images lead to great distances, remote worlds whose influences here converge. They talk first of Lena Lingard's Lapland grandmother (Did she wear skins? asks Jim). Then they recall the tales of the Spanish adventurers, Coronado and his search for the Seven Golden Cities. A sword with a Spanish inscription had been found in an adjoining county. It is then, with the Lapps and the Spaniards at our side, there we see the primordial image of the plow silhouetted against the circled gold of the sun—"heroic in size, a picture writing on the sun" (pp. 242–45). The ties of present and past are not stated, but felt. Out of her particular experience, she fused materials to suggest a world of many lives engaged in the recurring processes of history, the rise and fall of civilizations, of human endeavor.

At the end of *My Ántonia* Jim Burden returns to the plains of his childhood and to the road by which he came to that place. The tracks have almost disappeared, are "mere shadings in the grass." His sense is of coming home to himself, "and of having found out what a little circle man's experience is" (pp. 371–72). Jim's circle in time is of his own history and much of America's. The beginnings of his life on the new land are recorded only in fading trail marks on the grass, an image hauntingly like that other symbolic circle of life, the Indian trail he had once seen etched faintly in the snow.

NOTES

1. "Willa Cather Talks of Work" (*Philadelphia Record*, datelined 9 August 1913), in *The Kingdom of Art: Willa Cather's First Principles and Critical Statements, 1893*, selected and edited with an introduction and two essays by Bernice Slote (Lincoln: University of Nebraska Press, 1966), p. 488.

2. For short stories, pagination given in the text is to *Willa Cather's Collected Short Stories, 1892–1912*, edited by Virginia Faulkner with an introduction by Mildred R. Bennett, rev. ed. (Lincoln: University of Nebraska Press, 1970).

3. Willa Cather, *My Ántonia* (1918; reprint ed., Boston: Houghton Mifflin Co., Sentry Edition, 1954), p. i. Page references to Willa Cather's novels are given in the text to this and the following editions: *O Pioneers!* (1913; reprint ed., Boston: Houghton Mifflin Co., 1962) and *The Song of the Lark* (1915; reprint ed., Boston: Houghton Mifflin Co., 1943).

4. Willa Cather, "Nebraska: The End of the First Cycle," *Nation*, 5 September 1923, p. 237.

5. *Courier*, 25 December 1897, pp. 2–3; reprinted in *The World and the Parish: Willa Cather's Articles and Reviews, 1893–1902*, selected and edited by William M. Curtin, 2 vols. (Lincoln: University of Nebraska Press, 1970), 1:413–14.

6. Anson Uriel Hancock, *John Auburntop, Novelist* (Chicago: C. H. Kerr, 1891), pp. 184–85.

7. Lonnie Pierson, "Lyra and Silas Garber: A Nebraska Story" (M. A. thesis, University of Nebraska–Lincoln, 1977).

8. Willa Cather, *On Writing: Critical Studies of Writing as an Art*, with a foreword by Stephen Tennant (New York: Alfred A. Knopf, 1962), p. 41.

Part 3

Contemporary Minorities Blacks and Chicanos

CHESTER J. FONTENOT, JR.

Oscar Micheaux,
Black Novelist and Film Maker

OSCAR MICHEAUX, who lived from 1884 to 1951, was a black novelist and movie producer who believed that one solution to the problems that plagued black urbanites was for them to abandon the cities and to look to the Great Plains as a place where they could build an alternative society. Similarly, according to Micheaux, black southerners could homestead in what he called the Great Northwest (northern Great Plains) instead of following Booker T. Washington's philosophy of economic and moral betterment and staying in the South. Drawing upon his own experience as a settler on the Rosebud Reservation in South Dakota from 1909 to 1914, Micheaux delineated the process of blacks freeing themselves from urban decadence in each of his seven novels, but especially in *The Conquest* (1913), *The Forged Note* (1915), and *The Homesteader* (1917).[1]

Not only was Micheaux the first black writer to portray a black leading character in the role of a pioneer, he was also the first black film maker. He produced at least forty-five movies and organized private corporations to distribute both his films and his books. Micheaux tried to present a realistic picture of black urban life in contrast to that which then emanated from Hollywood studios. Instead of emphasizing

109

the carnal or gutter instinct of black people, he tried to portray the problems of the black middle class. Although he has been criticized for casting light-skinned people as actors in his films for imitating white society, and for using black people as plastic models, he sought to offer meaningful alternatives to the negative images created by the American film industry.

My purpose in this essay is to discuss Micheaux's three major novels and analyze briefly some of the things he attempted to do in his films. His significance for the study of Afro-American literature and films is clear enough. His philosophy is important because it led him to break through propagandistic notions about the social and political situation of Afro-Americans and because he moved black people from the category of subhuman creatures incapable of carrying out the most ordinary human functions to one of a dignified people whose problems are much like those of white Americans.

The stereotyping of black people in films as subhuman has a long history. In 1905, *Fights of Nations* and *The Wooing and Wedding of a Coon* showed blacks as childlike lackeys who were meant to be ridiculed. In 1907, *The Masher* told the story of a ladies' man who chased anyone remotely resembling a woman, but whose advances were always rebuffed; finally, he succeeds with a veiled lady, only to discover that she is a black woman. In 1910 and 1911, slapstick comedies—*Pickaninnies and Watermelon*, *Chicken Thief*, *Coon-Town Suffragettes*, *How Rastus Got His Turkeys*, *Rastus and Chicken*, *Rastus in Zululand*—stereotyped blacks as so completely illiterate that "they did not have to respond when demeaned because they were always unaware of what was being done."[2] The Sambo films, which appeared between 1909 and 1911, also offered stock racist black characters. In 1910, after the release of *Uncle Tom's Cabin*, came several films which characterized blacks as faithful slaves often so loyal to their masters that they would voluntarily offer themselves for sale rather than see their masters agonize over gambling debts. The image of Uncle Tom as faithful slave was developed in such films as *The Dark Romance of a To-*

bacco Can (1911), *For Massa's Sake* (1911), *The Debt* (1912), and *Slavery Days* (1913). Their enormous appeal to white audiences encouraged Hollywood producers to film stories of miscegenation, dealing with the tragic mulatto. For example, *The Nigger and the Octoroon* (1913), attached shame and degradation to even the smallest measure of nonwhite blood, thereby implying that being black was somehow subhuman.[3]

The acceptance of antiblack images in American films probably can be explained by the willingness of white Americans to see confirmed in visual images their belief that black people were subhuman. The Hollywood film industry, which had begun its quick rise to prominence, saw a chance to gain an economic foothold in American society by exploiting the tremendous mythmaking potential of motion pictures. Motion pictures exert a considerable influence on an audience partly because film is mimetic; that is, a film attempts to capture a selected version of reality. Since we see only what is selected for us by the camera, films unfold a story by narration. The camera gives the film an authorial presence much like that found in fiction; the movements of the camera constitute style. Like novels, films can render anything which can be perceived. A film presents speech through "techniques more vivid but conceptually equivalent to those of language. Just as the formal identity of fiction depends on the existence of narrated description as well as dialogue, so the formal identity of film is dependent upon its ability to describe experience through the medium of cinematography as well as to make statements about language."[4]

Micheaux understood the mythmaking potential both of novels and of films, and made use of these media in his attempt to create an alternate set of cultural referents for Afro-Americans. Since his films were based largely on his first three novels, a description of their plots is appropriate here.

Writing autobiographically about his life in western South Dakota, Micheaux invented three personae: Oscar Devereaux, Jean Baptiste, and Sidney Wyeth. In *The Conquest* Oscar Devereaux sets out to establish himself as a homesteader in South Dakota and to conquer the Northwest.

A good deal of the story told in *The Conquest* is repeated in greater detail in the story of Jean Baptiste in *The Homesteader*. In *The Forged Note* the hero is Sidney Wyeth, who has written a novel; he goes to Attalia (Atlanta) to promote its sale, sees the decadence of black urban life, and meets and marries a black woman. In each novel the protagonist is a black pioneer who sets out to create a new society free of the restrictions and distortions of life in urban areas. Viewed in this light, the novels represent an attempt to create a mythology, to construct an alternate set of values to that already existing in black urban society, and to depict this new mythology in a manner which would be accessible to black people in general.

Micheaux's mythology is thematic: *The Conquest* and *The Homesteader* stress the importance to black Americans of avoiding at all costs interracial marriage and of abandoning the cities for the Great Northwest; *The Forged Note* offers a critique of the most damaging aspects of black urban life. In writing these novels Micheaux wanted to reorder the cultural mores of black Americans, to transmute the decadence he found into a solid moral and intellectual cornerstone upon which black Americans could build a society free of the existing pitfalls.

The hero of *The Conquest*, Oscar Devereaux, is an enterprising young black man, determined to show that black people can do anything they want to do. Leaving his family at the age of sixteen, he takes a job paying $1.25 a day in a car-manufacturing company, where he meets a black minister, the Reverend McIntyre, described as a "fire-eating colored evangelist." Devereaux decides that the religious fervor of the black church is unproductive and ultimately antithetical to self-determination. After spending about two years in the car-manufacturing plant, he leaves for an all-black town. He gets a job boiling water in a coal mine for $2.25 a day, but since he sees no opportunity for advancement he moves on to Carbondale, Illinois, where his sister teaches school. She introduces him to a beautiful black girl, Jessie Ross, with whom he later becomes involved. Moving on again, this time to Chicago, he works part time at the Union Stockyards for

$1.50 a day. Dissatisfied with this situation, he goes to nearby Joliet to work in the steel mills. Here he is employed at the coal chutes at $1.50 per twenty-five tons of coal shoveled, but the work is much too severe for him. Returning to Chicago, he is swindled out of two dollars by an employment agency, and goes next to Eaton, where he works in a barbershop shining shoes. He takes on a second job working on a farm, but quits after one hard day of pitching hay with a sixteen-year-old girl and a second day of shucking oats with a twelve-year-old boy, a fourteen-year-old girl, and the farmer's wife. Concluding that manual labor is not for him, Devereaux finds employment with the Pullman Company on a parlor car that runs through summer resorts in southern Wisconsin. Eventually he becomes porter of his own car, the Altata. With his friend Wright he devises a scheme for swindling fares on the train. When his share of the profits amounts to $2,340, he goes west.

At this point, the plot begins to take shape. Devereaux hears about Oristown, South Dakota, a town on the edge of the Little Crow Reservation. Parts of the reservation are to be opened to settlement; would-be settlers are to draw lots for homesteads. Since there are only twenty-four homesteads available and about ten times that many people have placed their names in the lottery, it appears to Devereaux that his chances of obtaining a homestead are very remote— he holds number 6,540—and he starts back to Chicago. En route he learns that it is possible to buy a relinquished claim. Heartened by this news he returns to Oristown and finally succeeds in purchasing a relinquishment for $375. Being new to the Great Northwest and ignorant of its ways, Devereaux is an easy mark for horse-traders, who sell him their poorest stock at high prices, and for merchants, who sell him defective farm equipment. Nonetheless, he manages to turn over ten to twelve acres per year, winning the respect of his white neighbors. The greatest hardship he suffers is the lack of female companionship; there are almost no eligible black women in South Dakota. Since he wants to maintain racial loyalty, he visits Jessie Ross in Carbondale and declares that he loves her.

Upon his return to South Dakota, Devereaux buys a

neighboring homestead for three thousand dollars, but the acquisition of the additional land leaves him little time to court Jessie. During the period between their last meeting and his next trip to see Jessie, he meets and falls in love with a twenty-year-old Scottish girl, but decides against marrying her because of the color barrier. Still determined to find a suitable wife, Devereaux again seeks out Jessie Ross, but he is too late; during his long absence she has married someone else. His quest for a wife appears to be ended when he makes the acquaintance of Orlean McCarthy, the daughter of a black minister whom he had met when visiting Jessie. After a brief courtship he persuades Orlean to return to South Dakota with him and get married, but her father wants them to abide by social custom and be married in Chicago. Devereaux goes to Chicago to win her back, but is unsuccessful.

The story of *The Conquest* is rendered in more detail in *The Homesteader*. In this novel Oscar Devereaux becomes Jean Baptiste, the Scottish girl is called Agnes Stewart, and Orlean McCarthy retains the same name. The plot moves quickly into thematic categories. In an overly sentimental scene Baptiste and Agnes meet and fall in love, but before Baptiste can make up his mind to marry her he recalls the story of a black man who married a white woman and ended up claiming to be Mexican, not black. The recollection of this story impels Baptiste to give up the idea of marrying Agnes. Committed to marrying within his race, he goes to Chicago, meets Orlean McCarthy, and embarks upon a fiery courtship. We learn that her father, the Reverend McCarthy, is sexually promiscuous and that he has plotted to keep Orlean from marrying Baptiste. But his scheming is thwarted: Baptiste marries Orlean and takes her to live on his homestead. He buys the neighboring homestead for his bride, but the purchase is challenged by the townspeople. When news of their problems reaches the Reverend McCarthy, he visits Baptiste and Orlean, who is now pregnant, and starts to plant the seeds which will eventually destroy their marriage. After McCarthy returns to Chicago, Baptiste leaves the homestead for a few days and during his absence the baby is born dead. Orlean's father seizes the opportunity to break up the marriage and takes Orlean back to Chicago.

Baptiste and Orlean do not see each other for a year; then they are reunited in Chicago and he hopes that she will return with him to the homestead. When he gets into an argument with her father, Orlean attacks Baptiste viciously and he allows her to beat him up. Back in South Dakota Baptiste faces a drought and is soon in deep financial trouble. He loses his own land but is saved by his sister's homestead, which is not in his name and thus is not legally subject to foreclosure. In the face of adversity, Baptiste resolves to become a writer. He has a book published and sets up a publishing house.

Now Micheaux launches his criticism of black urban society. Baptiste engages Irene Grey, a mulatto woman to whom he once wrote letters, to help him sell his books. He is impressed by her and her father, Junius N. Grey, known as the Negro Potato King, and sees in them the prototypes of the black race. The juxtaposition of Irene and Junius Grey with Orlean and the Reverend McCarthy is significant, for Baptiste perceives that the oppression of the black people is not wholly the fault of the whites; contributing factors are the inability to read and the generally decadent nature of urban black people. In particular, Baptiste criticizes black Baptist ministers like McCarthy for their lack of education. Moreover, he attributes much of the conflict between Orlean's father and himself to different ideologies: Baptiste is a follower of Booker T. Washington, while the Reverend McCarthy subscribes to the ideas of W. E. B. Dubois. McCarthy uses his ideology so effectively that he alienates Orlean from her love for Baptiste, causes her to sell the homestead Baptiste has given her, and unwittingly sets up a situation which ends in her committing patricide and suicide. Baptiste is accused of the double murder but is acquitted, thanks to a detective who succeeds in solving the case. He is then reunited with Agnes Stewart, who has become an established songwriter. They discover that she is a mulatto, resolving the tension created by the prospect of interracial marriage, and become man and wife.

The interwoven theme of these two novels is most clearly seen in Micheaux's exposé of the vices of black urban life. He contrasts the harsh reality of that life—violence, racism, lack of education, unemployment, black-on-black crime—with the utopian environment of the Great Northwest. In *The Conquest* and *The Homesteader* Micheaux sets up the first parts of his mythology: loyalty to the black race (dramatized in the rejection of interracial marriage) and black settlement of the Great Northwest.

In *The Forged Note* Micheaux itemizes the destructive elements of black city life. Devereaux / Baptiste is reborn as Sidney Wyeth, the black author of a novel called *The Tempest*. In order to increase sales Wyeth travels to several cities hiring agents who will promote the book. In Atlanta his eyes are opened to the degradation of black life in the cities, a situation which he blames on the failure of blacks to read black literature (or, for that matter, much of any literature). From Atlanta he goes to Effingham (Birmingham), where illiteracy is even more rampant. He comments that "these people considered literature, as a whole, dead stock. More than sixty thousand in number, the demand among them for books and magazines was insufficient to justify anyone's running a place for such a purpose. It was not large enough to justify either of the Negro drug stores carrying periodicals in stock, even those that were carried by all white drug stores, excepting those in districts occupied and patronized by the colored people" (p. 324). Black people seemed to be more interested in establishing an all-black park than in building a library in a black community. Wyeth sees a great part of the corruption of youth as stemming from lack of interest in education, but he does not blame blacks entirely. He believes that civilization is an artificial construct which does not permit the individual to grow from his own potential. In this sense Micheaux is almost Rousseauesque. He thinks the Great Northwest will allow black people to build an alternate society which will annihilate the social and racial distinctions that are the foundation of urban society. This seems to indicate that Micheaux does not adhere strictly to Booker T. Wahington's philosophy, for Washington believed that blacks should remain in the South and try to gain an economic foothold, while Micheaux sees the South as corrupt and beyond redemption. The alternative, then, is to leave both artificial worlds—the North and the South—and settle in a region untainted by American racism.

The faults of black leaders are personified in Micheaux's characterizations of black ministers. Orlean's father, the Reverend McCarthy, is guilty of much worse offenses than hypocrisy; he uses the office of the church for his own benefit. Mildred Latham, the black woman whom Sidney Wyeth falls in love with and marries, is tormented by the knowledge that her father took five thousand dollars of his church's money and used it to be made a bishop. The ranks of black leadership comprise uneducated ministers, a few teachers who also share a dislike of black literature, and a couple of self-styled politicians. Wyeth becomes so disgusted with black leaders that he is responsible for the appearance of the following headline in a black southern newspaper: "NEGRO SAYS RACE FACES DREADFUL CONDITIONS, DUE TO LACK OF LEADERS. SAYS SELFISHNESS IS SO MUCH THE ORDER THAT THERE IS NO INTEREST WHATEVER TOWARD UPLIFT. PROFESSIONAL NEGRO THE WORST."

Hugh M. Gloster writes that in *The Homesteader*, "though indicating the degeneracy of negro life in Southern cities, Micheaux offers no panacea and fails to exhibit the optimism and enterprise which characterize *The Conquest*."[5] This statement indicates a misreading, for while it is true that in *The Conquest* Micheaux does not condemn black urban life to the extent that he does in *The Homesteader* and *The Forged Note*, it is not because he is more optimistic in the earlier novel. Rather, he is investigating a different aspect of the mythology he is trying to construct. The purpose of *The Conquest* is to show that the black race can determine its own destiny, that it can leave behind the moral decadence of cities, and that it can build a more suitable society in the Great Northwest. Speaking through the voice of Oscar Devereaux, Micheaux says: "For years I have felt constrained to deplore the negligence of the colored race in America, in not seizing the opportunity for monopolizing more of the many million acres of rich farm lands in the great Northwest, where immigrants from the old world own many acres of rich farm lands, while the millions of blacks, only a few hundred miles away, are as oblivious to it all as the heathen of Africa are to civilization" (p. 204).

In contrast, *The Forged Note* is Micheaux's attempt to lead the black reader from the decadent world of black urban life to the liberated life of the Great Northwest. He chooses to do this through focusing on the evils existing in black southern life and pointing to some possible reasons for their coming into existence. True, he does not offer a panacea for the problems he exposes, for ready-made solutions are as artificial as the civilization whites have imposed upon blacks. Like Voltaire's Candide, the black race must learn to work toward a realistic goal, not an abstract one such as that described in the ideology of W. E. B. Dubois. The process of ridding the black race of the weaknesses which prevent natural growth goes through several stages: rejection of interracial marriage, acceptance of moral responsibilities, and embracing education through literature.

Micheaux's efforts to popularize his novels led him into film making. Since 1913, when he established the Western Book and Supply Company in Sioux City, Iowa, Micheaux had been able to reach a large audience. In 1918 George P. Johnson, general booking agent of the black-owned-and-operated Lincoln Film Company of Los Angeles, read *The Homesteader*, and through the company's Omaha office got in touch with Micheaux to see about the possibility of producing it. At a meeting in Omaha in May 1918, Micheaux signed a contract with Johnson which provided that he would go to Los Angeles and watch the filming of his novel. But Micheaux's desire to supervise the filming and his total lack of experience in directing led to the cancellation of the contract.

In the latter part of 1918 Micheaux formed the Micheaux Film and Book Company, with offices in Sioux City and Chicago.[6] As he had done previously, when he established the Western Book and Supply Company, Micheaux sold stock in the new company to white farmers around Sioux City and finally amassed sufficient capital to make an eight-reel film of *The Homesteader*.

Subsequently, he produced more than forty-four black-cast films nationally, some of which were also distributed in Europe. They achieved such wide distribution partly because of Micheaux's refusal to indulge in propagandizing. In his view, black people did not want racial propaganda of the sort that characterized many films produced by Hollywood and by some white independents. He believed that a good story was what they wanted, and a good story must mirror reality, reflecting accurately the social, economic, and political conditions common to the lives of American black people. Though some of his productions may be considered protest films, he did not see film solely as a political instrument. The mythology which he stressed attempted to combat the unrealistic images of black people created by Hollywood producers, images which Donald Bogle identifies as toms, coons, mulattoes, mammies, and bucks.[7]

In an article published in the *Philadelphia Afro-American* (24 January 1925), Micheaux discussed his approach to film making. Film, Micheaux observes, is an art which requires an extraordinary amount of "encouragement and financial backing," neither of which he had been able to obtain in abundance. A black producer dares to "step into a world which has hitherto remained closed to him. His entrance into this unexplored field, is for him, trebly difficult. He is united [*sic*] in his themes, in obtaining casts that present genuine ability, and in his financial resources." Micheaux's comments on the extra difficulties confronting black film producers were not meant to shield his own work from criticism. "I do not wish anyone to construe this as a request for suppression of criticism," he states. "Honest, intelligent criticism is an aid to the progress of any effort. The producer who has confidence in his ideals solicits constructive criticism. But he also asks fairness, and fairness in criticism demands a familiarity with the aims of the producer, and a knowledge of the circumstances under which his efforts were materialized."

Many of Micheaux's critics apparently feel no need to respond to his plea to take into account the exceptional difficulties under which he labored or to consider his films from the point of view of their creator's conscious intention. Disregarding these two factors, they are too willing to write off his productions as second-rate underground films, comparable to Hollywood C-grade productions. After Micheaux released a seven-reel feature, *The Dungeon*, D. Ireland Thomas, writing in the *Chicago Defender* (8 July 1922), castigated him for using light-skinned actors and for not giving the film "race" promotion: "The advertising matter for this production has nothing to indicate that the feature is colored, as the characters are very bright [*sic*]; in fact almost white. 'The All-Star Colored Cast' that is so noticeable with nearly every race production is omitted on the cards and lithographs. Possibly Mr. Micheaux is relying on his name alone to tell the public that it is a race production or maybe he is after booking it in white theaters."

D. Ireland Thomas's criticism of Micheaux is typical of that of the majority of his critics. Even those who temper their comments with a tribute do so by way of an apologia. An article in the *Baltimore Afro-American* (24 July 1921) exemplifies this sort of qualified praise. It attacks race movie fans for their failure to develop separate criteria for evaluating black-produced films. And since the development of race films was in an embryonic state in 1921, harsh criticism from the audience was a threat to the survival of the new genre: "Moving pictures cannot be made without money. These pictures are shown in houses catering to colored patrons only. From them must come the means that will determine whether the industry will live. To bear with such men as Oscar Micheaux and other pioneers today means bigger and better race pictures tomorrow."

Some critics did evaluate Micheaux's works from the perspective of his conscious intention, but—ironically—it was partly because of such criticism that several of his films were nearly banned from public showing in Chicago and Philadelphia. In the previously cited 1925 article, Micheaux wrote that his intention was to "present the truth, to lay before the race a cross section of its own life, to view the colored heart from close range." He believed that "it is only by presenting those portions of the race portrayed in my pictures, in the light and background of their true state, that we can raise our people to greater heights. I am too much involved with the spirit of Booker T. Washington to engraft false virtues upon ourselves, to make ourselves that which we are not."

The false virtues of which he speaks are usually portrayed in his films as vices associated with black urban life. It is important to realize that many of the stereotypes Micheaux was fighting were propagated by black as well as white producers and writers. Micheaux's depiction of black people was also in striking contrast to the images popularized by the writers of the Harlem Renaissance. Many black writers of the 1920s tended to glorify the black lower class (pimps, whores, pushers, and so on), and to denigrate the black middle class as imitation white people. Moreover, black writers who attempted to reverse negative images of black people by elevating the "dregs of society" (to paraphrase Frantz Fanon) to "humanly" status insisted that the low-life characters they created were representative of black culture.

Micheaux was not alone in his criticism of the tendency to place one aspect of black life on a symbolic level intended to represent the whole; George Schuyler also made a critical analysis of the reversal of images by black writers. To my knowledge, however, Micheaux was the only black artist to present his critique through the medium of cinema. Unlike those black writers of the Harlem Renaissance who stigmatized black middle-class people as plastic replicas of white society incapable of sustaining African and Afro-American cultural traditions, Micheaux portrayed the black middle class as real people who were well educated, whose moral standards were high, and who were strongly motivated to achieve success. However, the methods by which members of that class attempted to better themselves often led them to commit dishonest or criminal acts, even murder. The plots of many of Micheaux's films center on realistic problems of the black middle class.

While Micheaux's emphasis on plot derived in part from his belief that black people wanted a good story, he had to depend on story because he lacked the technical ability to create special effects and the financial resources required to stage massive, spectacular action scenes. He usually did all the work on his productions, except for minor tasks: he wrote the scenarios, supervised filming, and handled the bookkeeping. His pictures took an average of ten days to shoot and usually cost ten to twelve thousand dollars. The most remarkable thing about Micheaux's career both as a novelist and as a film maker was his ability to work within stringent limitations. He rarely would reshoot a scene, no matter how badly it turned out, and as substitutes for a studio he used the homes and offices of his friends.

Quite often Micheaux would grant a theater manager first rights to show his films in return for the money to make them. In quest of such a deal, he would visit prospective patrons accompanied by several actors. The actors would perform a couple of scenes for the theater manager and Micheaux would extol the importance and marketability of the script.

In 1920 Micheaux's brother, Swan, joined him as manager of the Micheaux Film and Book Company; later he was promoted to secretary-treasurer and general manager. In 1921, when the corporation had a 25 percent cash dividend, it opened an office in New York, where facilities were better and casting easier; however, the distribution and financial office remained in Chicago under the supervision of Swan Micheaux and Charles Benson. Tiffany Tolliver and W. R. Crowell distributed the Micheaux films in the East from a branch office in Roanoke, Virginia, and A. Odams, owner of the Verdun Theatre in Beaumont, Texas, was the distributor for the Southwest. Lack of money forced Micheaux to file a voluntary petition in 1928. At this time the Micheaux Film Company listed assets of $1,400 and liabilities of $7,837. Yet Micheaux's perseverance, combined with the ingenuity of Alice Russell, an actress he married in 1929, soon got him back in business. Having obtained new money, he reorganized the company in the latter half of 1929, incorporating it under New York state laws.

Between 1918 and 1931 Micheaux produced twenty-seven films, most of them silent. His first all-sound feature was *The Exile* (1931), another adaptation of *The Homesteader*. Between 1931 and 1940 he produced and directed sixteen all-sound features. His last known film activity was writing and directing *The Betrayal* (1948), adapted from his novel *The Wind from Nowhere*. It opened to poor reviews in a white movie theater in downtown New York. Three years later, in 1951, Micheaux died at the age of sixty-seven in Charlotte, North Carolina.

Although Micheaux operated independently, a good many of his critics seek to equate his productions with those Hollywood made for blacks. Eileen Landry writes that Micheaux's stories were "often typically Hollywood—adventures, melodramas, mysteries—starring black actors. There was little 'ethnic truth' to these films; Micheaux gave his audiences a 'black Valentino' and a 'sepia Mae West.' And he perpetuated many white stereotypes; his heroes and heroines were usually light-skinned and fine-featured, his villains darker and more negroid. While some of his films dealt with the problem of being black, this was never from the point of view of the ghetto dweller or sharecropper; his subjects were the black bourgeoisie."[8]

The same sort of comments have been made by those among Micheaux's critics who fail to place his books and films within the parameters of his conscious intention. Such criticism also omits from consideration the strongest characters Micheaux created—black pioneers. For it was through the creation of the black pioneer as an individual able to collapse the distinction between race and class that Micheaux made his most lasting contribution to black literature and films. The black pioneer is freed from the artifices of "civilization" and is allowed to fulfill his own potential through a process inherent in his cultural history.

Oscar Micheaux is emblematic of the black pioneer as a symbol of black achievement. The character was derived from experiences he himself had lived through. His films explore various aspects of the problem of being black in a racially oriented society from the point of view of black goal-oriented behavior. Central to the mythology he constructed in his novels and popularized in his films is the emphasis on abandoning metropolitan black areas and moving to the Great Northwest, where black men and women could build a civilization based on their own cultural ethos. Micheaux's impact on black film is widely recognized, even though its nature is debated. His film making stands as a symbol of the race pride he sought to instill in black people through his emphasis on the values of the black middle class.

NOTES

1. Oscar Micheaux, *The Conquest: The Story of a Negro Pioneer* (Lincoln, Nebr.: Woodruff Press, 1913); *The Homesteader* (College Park, Md.: McGrath Publishing Co., 1969, c. 1917); *The Forged Note; A Romance of the Darker Races* (Lincoln, Nebraska: Western Book Supply, (1915). Later novels are *The Wind from Nowhere* (1944), *The Case of Mrs. Wingate* (1945), *The Story of Dorothy Stanfield* (1946), and *The Masquerade: An Historical Novel* (1947), all published by the New York Book Supply Company. Despite the magnitude of Micheaux's contribution to black literature, he has been curiously neglected by Afro-American scholars. Addison Gayle, Jr., in his massive study of the Afro-American novel, *The Way of the New World: The Black Novel in America* (Garden City, New York: Anchor Press, 1975), does not even mention Micheaux; Robert A. Bone, in *The Negro Novel in America* (New Haven: Yale University Press, 1958), refers to him in passing as one "who plays white as children play house"; Roger Whitlow gives him a paragraph in *Black American Literature: A Critical History* (Chicago: Nelson Hall, 1973); and Hugh M. Gloster devotes but five pages to him in *Negro Voices in American Fiction* (Chapel Hill: University of North Carolina Press, 1948) and lists only three of his novels.

2. Donald Bogle, *Toms, Coons, Mulattoes, Mammies and Bucks* (New York: Viking Press, 1973), pp. 109–16.

3. Peter Noble, *The Negro in Films* (London: S. Robinson, 1948), p. 29.

4. Charles Thomas Samuels, *Mastering the Film and Others Essays* (Knoxville: University of Tennessee Press, 1977), p. 12.

5. Gloster, *Negro Voices in American Fiction,* p. 87.

6. For pertinent information about the Micheaux Film and Book Company, I am indebted to Henry T. Sampson, *Blacks in Black and White: A Source Book on Black Films* (Metuchen, New Jersey: Scarecrow Press, 1977), pp. 42–56. This is an excellent source book for specific details about black films. I have also relied on it heavily for listings of Micheaux's films and for critical commentary referred to in this essay.

7. Bogle, *Toms, Coons, Mulattoes, Mammies and Bucks,* pp. 109–16.

8. Eileen Landry, *Black Film Stars* (New York: Drake Publishing Co., 1973), p. 45.

TOMÁS RIVERA

The Great Plains as Refuge in Chicano Literature

THE GREAT PLAINS have a special attraction to me as a person and as a fiction writer. I spent half of my first twenty years in one or another midwestern or Great Plains state. As a child and as a young man, I lived in Iowa, the Dakotas, Minnesota, Michigan, Wisconsin, and Ohio. My earliest recollections are of waking up on a farm in northern Minnesota close to the North Dakota border, where my parents and other relatives worked in the beet fields, surrounded by sounds that I hear even today. These sounds of the farm animals and the voices of working men continue to have a distinct and almost unique clarity and quality. I am beginning this essay in this very personal manner because I think that literature is a personal endeavor—whether you write it or read it.

The second largest migration of Mexican-Americans into what we called *el norte* occurred during the late 1920s and '30s. My parents and other relatives were among that group. Actually, we had ventured out of Texas in the years just before World War II; the largest migration came during the course of the war.

As a child I became aware of various differences between the people we worked for in Texas and the people we worked with in *el norte.* Perhaps just here in these words—worked *for* and worked *with*—is the main difference. Other differences that I noted were linguistic; in *el norte* I would hear languages other than English. I first realized what an immigrant was in the late 1940s in Duncan, Iowa. Previously, I had read some elementary historical accounts of how the great American experience had drawn together people from all over the world, but to me the first real immigrant was Peter Falada, a member of the Czech colony in Duncan. Upon our arrival he asked us one question: "When did your folks come over from the Old Country?" I was born in Texas and we were then spending half the year in the Midwest or the Dakotas, so, although we were strangers to Iowa, I had never considered myself an immigrant. But my father said, "I came from the Old Country in 1915." "We beat you by five years," was Falada's reply. For the first time I saw my father as an immigrant.

That summer I began to discover other immigrant groups who had settled in this small town in north-central Iowa—Dutch, Swedes, Finns, and others. I also succeeded in getting Peter Falada and my father to talk of their experiences when they left "the Old Country" and came to the United States. They enjoyed profoundly telling tales of risks, hardships, survival, and of the challenges that earlier settlers faced with them. When we spoke in Spanish Peter Falada would become irritated and would remind us that we were in America. Then he would turn to his wife and children and speak in Czech, and they would all laugh. Our turn to be angry and our turn to tell them that they, too, were in America.

The annual experience of living away from a home base in Texas afforded me grounds for comparison when I developed my own ideas about environment and people. Economic necessity forced us to travel to places away from home and to come into contact with the inhabitants. Although the working conditions were hard, once we were back in Texas we could romanticize about the good land, *el norte.*

In freshman English I was introduced to what was later to be called ethnic literature. In the middle 1950s I had set out to search for, and perhaps find, something written by my own people. I was thirsty for descriptions that would reveal the hardships of a people who were searchers of work like us. Then, as part of a class assignment, I read *Giants in the Earth*. I am sure my professor was astonished by my interest and my desire to dwell on immigrant hardships and the naturalism of the novel, by my interpretations emphasizing the dignity of the common man, and—despite Rølvaag's specific ambience—the universality of the struggle. What my professor regarded as a vicarious experience on my part was a reliving and reconstruction of our own experience: as migrant workers in the forties and fifties, the Chicanos were giants in the earth. It was after reading Rølvaag that I decided I would one day tell the story of the Chicano migrant workers. The land, the people of the plains, and their drive to gain sustenance from the earth became a profound preoccupation.

Chicano literature has a deeply rooted tradition of intellectual emancipation. The myriad of underlying themes which focus on this tradition reveal the constant struggle to decolonize the mind of the Chicano. There is need to show a struggle, there is need to conserve a culture, and there is need to portray the Chicano as a whole human being, with all the frailties, virtues, and faults common to every man.

Among the many themes in Chicano literature that speak to the migrant experience is the concept of refuge. The refuge may be the family, a cultural home base, the Spanish language, the food, Mexican customs. At times, refuge is the idealistic notion of a more or less perfect culture that has ended, the cultural mystique of a past of pageantry, pomp, and learning. Then there is the refuge, mostly economic, that a migrant people seeks. For the seasonal migrant worker, the Great Plains was this kind of refuge. As Chicano literature interprets that aspect of Chicano life, several writers attempting to capture and document the experiences of the thirties, forties, and fifties depict the Great Plains variously as a utopia, a free state, as a place of exploitation, transient jobs, and exhausting work, and as a desolate and impersonal region that drove one to turn inward. The people as well as the environment deserve to be written about, for life in the Great Plains is a solid part of the Chicano experience. The region was a place to go once you had made a decision that it was also your country, and once you sensed you also had a future.

For the Chicano and for the Mexican of the latter half of the twentieth century, migration to the United States is a political, economic, and social act. Speaking of the exodus from Mexico to the deserts of the southwestern United States and a step farther on into the heartland, Ernesto Galarza, one of the foremost Chicano essayists, says: "It was not to flee the revolution as much as to flee their aftermath of defeat and frustration, that the landless came." In his analysis of the land system and social injustices that caused the migrations of millions, Galarza calls the exodus one of the great movements in history:

> Migration is the failure of roots. Displaced men are ecological victims. Between them and the sustaining earth a wedge has been driven. Eviction by drouths or dispossession by landlords, the impoverishment of the soil or conquest by arms, nature and man, separately or together, lay down the choice: move or die. . . . The Mexicans who left their homeland in the six decades beginning in 1880 represented one of the major mass movements of people in the western hemisphere.[1]

The power, the material advancement, the sense of oneness with the human race which these migrants sought is a constant dream even to the present time. Although the great majority settled in California and Texas, a large segment went on into the Midwest. The three basic enclaves of Mexican Americans today are in Texas and California and Chicago.

The sense of drive and movement is caught realistically in the work of the renowned anthropologist Manuel Gamio, writing in the 1930s. In the real-life story of one Mexican's travel and experiences, *The Personal Narration of Elías Garza,* he describes the transition from the Mexican to the Mexican-American experience:

> At that time I heard there were many good jobs here in the United States and that good money could be made. Some other

friends accompanied me and we went first to Mexico City and
from there we came to Ciudad Juarez. We then went to El Paso
and there we took a *renganche* [contract] to Kansas. We worked
on the tracks, taking up and laying down the rails, removing
the old ties and putting in new, and doing all kinds of hard
work. They only paid us $1.50 and exploited us without mercy
in the Commissary camp, for they sold us everything high.
Nevertheless, as at that time things were cheap, I managed to
make a little money with which I went back to La Piedad to see
my mother.[2]

Chicano literature covering the migrations of the late
nineteenth and twentieth centuries treats three basic types
of worker: the *vaquero* (cowboy), the *trasquilador* (sheep
shearer), and the *traquero, trabajador del traque* (railroad
hand). As Tomás Ybarra-Frausto states in his study "Cuando
vino el alambre, vino el hambre" (When the [barbed] wire
came, came the hunger):

The life and experiences of these men who left an indelible
imprint on the early Southwest [the Midwest and the Great
Plains] are reflected in various forms of literary expression.
They had their poets, their composers, and their makers of
legends whose *corridoes* [ballads], *coplas* [couplets], and stories
distill the essence of their experience. The basis of their literary
expression was a rich vocabulary dealing with the new
phenomena they constantly came upon.[3]

During the 1800s approximately 70 percent of the section
crews and 90 percent of the extra gangs (temporary replace-
ments) on some railroad lines were composed of Mexican
laborers, legally and illegally hired by agents of contractors.

"Los reenganchados a Kansas" (Contracted to Kansas) is
a *corrido* about the thousands of men who traveled accompanied by their families and lived in boxcars while working
on the track for the Santa Fe, the Rock Island, the Great
Northern, or the Southern Pacific. Many of the present colonies and barrios, especially in the Great Plains, were originally settled by this group of migrants and immigrants who
preceded the major migration of 1910. The *corrido,* in part,
goes like this:

One day the third of September,
Oh, what an unusual day!
We left Laredo
Signed up for Kansas. . . .

One of my companions
Shouted very excitedly:
"Now we are going under contract
To work for cash."

Run, run little machine
Along the Katy line,
Carry this party of laborers
To the State of Kansas City. . . .

The final stanza of the *corrido* presents the Mexican view of U.S. labor unions as having a double standard. The *reenganchados* knew that since they were not citizens of the United States they would receive no union benefits and were regarded simply as a means of increasing the numerical strength of the railroad unions, not as participating members.

From the turn of the century into the thirties, migration is an important theme in Chicano literature; indeed, it continues to be an important element in the 1970s.[4] In 1976 the Chicano writer Rolando Hinojosa-Smith received the Premio Casa de las Américas for the best novel. That Hinojosa should be awarded this prestigious prize, never before given to a North American, stands as a distinct achievement for Chicano literature. His novel, *Klail City y sus alrededores* (Klail City and its surroundings), devotes some thirty pages to the joy and hope and agony and disillusionment of traveling, working, and confrontation in the Great Plains and the Midwest.[5] One young man, P. Galindo, a native of Texas Valley, has an idealized notion of what to expect, even though he has previously traveled to *el norte* and sought work there. He is confident that he will find work and that everything will turn out well. One chapter deals with the death of a young woman's parents in Cheyenne Wells, Colorado, and the lonely journey of the bereaved through western Kansas and eastern Colorado. In search of refuge, they have found death.

Another character, the young man Gavira, has a truck which he names *El Rapido de Oklahoma* (The Oklahoma Express). He paints the name on his truck and is himself called by that name. Oklahoma has a touch of the exotic to the people in Texas Valley—that is, to the characters in the novel.

Throughout the novel (which actually is a collection of cameos lightly threaded together), as a unifying device, Hinojosa attacks the Anglos bitterly and sarcastically. George Markham, Big Foot Parkinson, Van Meers, and Mrs. Elsinore, all Texans, are shown as grotesque, one-dimensional creatures. The author balances his characterizations of Texas Anglos, however, by portraying a midwesterner, Tom Purdy, as the epitome of goodness. He describes Tom thus:

> This man without any money, but with dedication and determination, without having anyone come and whisper in his ear, said: "Enough; no more"; and he began to repair the houses available for the Chicano migrants. . . . He didn't talk to the federal or state government nor the press. Nor did he talk to those civic organizations that abound in almost every town in this country. No. He spoke with his wife and the two of them in silence and without hesitation began their chore for a group of people whom they didn't know and whose language they didn't speak. . . . What was accomplished allowed La Raza to live with dignity.

One of the most important elements in Chicano oral history and oral literature is the *corrido,* the ballad. Just as Spanish literature has its roots in the romance, so Chicano literature takes its basic design from the concrete, simple narrative of this art form. Luis Valdez calls the *corridos* the songs of Exodus. He states: " 'Wherever you go, you shall go singing,' the War God of the Aztecs, Huitzilopochtili, commanded the people. With the *corridos* of the Southwest La Raza has been singing its history ever since."[6] The songs of Exodus are many. Most are laments at leaving behind a country, a family, a loved one. Then there are those *corridos,* such as the songs of the vaqueros, in which the poet expresses his own response to new experiences and new landscapes. For the purpose of this essay I will confine my discussion to *corridos* dealing with the hard life of the vaquero. "The *Corrido* of Kansas" focuses on the imminent presence of death and the dangers of the two-month cattle drive from Texas to Kansas. Its last stanzas describe the death of a young vaquero.

> The wife of Alberto Flores
> Comes up to ask the foreman,
> "Where has my son stayed,
> For I have not seen him arrive?"
>
> "Ma'am, if I were to tell you
> You would start to weep;
> Your son was killed by a bull
> On the gates of a corral.
>
> "Thirty pesos was his wages
> But it was all owed.
> And I have put in three hundred
> To have him buried.
>
> "All the drivers
> Went to accompany him.
> With hats in hand
> They saw him buried.
>
> "And now I say farewell
> With thoughts of my beloved.
> We come also to the end
> Of this cattle-driving song."[7]

The scene at the end of the *corrido* is Kansas. All the elements of humanity and dignity refer to the place where the tragedy occurred.[8] What makes the many variants of the *corridos de Kiansis* so appealing to the vaqueros themselves? Is it because Kansas represents a goal? Economic gain? As a land far away from Texas Valley, is it an exotic place in the mind of the composer? Perhaps all of these.[9]

According to the renowned Mexican-American folklorist Américo Paredes, the cattle drives to Kansas were the inspiration for the oldest complete *corridos* from the lower Rio Grande border. They are among the oldest even in the Greater Mexican tradition. In his *Texas-Mexican Cancionero,* Paredes writes:

Everyone has heard of the famous cattle drives to Kansas, the subject of many a Western. What is not so well known is that it was cattle owned by Mexicans and Texas-Mexicans (some legally obtained from them and some not) that formed the bulk of the herds driven north from the Nueces–Rio Grande area, the so-called cradle of the cattle industry in the United States. Not all cattle that went north were driven by Anglo cowboys. Many of the trail drivers were Mexicans, some taking their own herds, other working for Anglo outfits. The late 1860s and early 1870s was a period when a good many Mexicans still were *dueños* on the Texas side. In this respect they could meet the Anglo on something like equal terms. But the Texas-Mexican possessed something else that gave him a certain status—the tools and the techniques of the vaquero trade, in which the Anglo was merely a beginner. The Mexican with some justice could feel superior to the Anglo when it came to handling horses and cattle, or facing occupational hazards such as flooded rivers. These attitudes were apparent in the *corridos* about the cattle drives to Kansas, pronounced "Kiansis" by Border rancheros.[10]

No doubt intercultural conflict is reflected in the many variants of the *corridos de Kiansis,* but what is of greater significance is, first, that the conflict is expressed in professional rivalries rather than in violence between men of different cultures; second, that in Kansas the Mexican could meet the Anglo on equal terms; and third, that the Kansas-Mexican experience elevated the status of the Texas-Mexican because he had the tools and knew the techniques of the vaquero trade. Since the *Kiansis corridos* make no mention of armed conflict between Mexicans and Anglos, the oral tradition at least conveyed to the Texas-Mexican that a different kind of justice prevailed in the Great Plains. There were no armed forays against an unarmed people.

The migrant worker who came after the era of the cattle drive found a similar situation. Time after time Chicano literature tells how the small farmer from the Midwest and Great Plains is different from the Texas farmer. Certainly there is a historical reason for this difference. Armed conflict did not occur in the Great Plains as a result of regional or national politics; Great Plains settlers are themselves recent

immigrants. But clearly it was working the land side by side
with the person who owned it that pleased and gave dignity to
the Mexican common laborer. It surprised the Mexicans that
not only did the men who owned the land join them in the
fields, but also the women. They were surprised to be invited
to eat in the farmers' homes. In fact, the working of the land is
a common denominator. The word filters back to Texas:[11] In
the Midwest and the Great Plains a person's worth is determined by the amount of hard work he or she can do. Even
children were able to understand this basic difference. In a
short story of mine called "Los niños no se aguantaron" (The
children were victims), a child longs to be up north rather
than in Texas. The elemental need for water draws him to his
death. He is shot "accidentally" by a Texas rancher for drinking water out of a cattle tank.[12]

The Great Plains is represented as a region where fair
play is at least more common and where the natural environment, though harsh, is fought by all alike. A sense of
isolation pervades Chicano literature set in the Great Plains.
There are stories of the aimless wandering of a penniless
family in search of work,[13] of illness striking a whole area, of
truck accidents, of exploitation, of floods or droughts that
prevent men from working, of hate. However, it is not hate
directed at any one person but at an endless cycle of poverty,
as in the poem "Odio" (Hatred), in which the poet sees the
Chicanos as weeds.[14]

> Weeds rupture the marble
> And I laugh at the whiteness.
> Alone,
> daggers,
> knifing,
> soundless,
> unloved through death.
> Torn from the earth,
> left to dry,
> to die.
>
> Future in the seed.
>
> Stone upon stone
> of despair.

      Stone from which
      come the weeds
      who blade each other
      without love

              to be torn from the earth
              and thrown to the earth.

      The seed is here
      on the stove
      on my forehead.

Similar in setting is the poem, "The Child Cried," by Javier Aréchiga,[15] which exalts the hopelessness and feeling of futility of a common field laborer:

      The child cried
      No one noticed
      He tried to hold
      But no one would help him
      He wanted water
      The others kept picking
      He felt burned from the sun
      Everybody was a picture
      He died.

If migrant workers remained in the Midwest or Great Plains, they usually moved from rural to urban areas. In the next two poems Aréchiga illustrates the fear, the indifference, and the loneliness not only of death but also of the unheeding urban steel mills.

              Perdido (Lost)

      I cried to what was
      I saw nothing but concrete,
      Rotten paper and wood not
      identifiable in the iron smoke

      We screamed by ourselves
      Panicking constantly,
      Still there was nothing.

      Many young swept with the big
      Smack.
      Forgotten by La Malinche. . . .[16]

La Bruja (The Witch)

She appeared so mysteriously
without warning and waiting
without compassion
without

Clanging, clanging and steel
the grinding, grinding of machinery
without warning and waiting
without love
without compassion
without

She uncovered herself
sickness attacking . . .

Ringing, ringing of noise
The floating, floating of faith
the injuries

She disappeared
knowing that all had been accomplished.

The Chicano literary movement of the last decade swept from west to east, starting in California and ending in Texas. A midwestern Chicano enclave also made its presence felt; in Gary, Indiana, the *Revista Chicano Riqueña* began to flourish in the early seventies. I mention this to illustrate an inherent cultural attitude on the part of the Chicano. The educational institutions of the Midwest and, to some degree, of the Great Plains, although not seriously attacked by Chicano students, felt the reverberations of conflicts in the Southwest.[17] The Chicano student who was becoming increasingly aware of his own historical traditions and who was confronted by the demands of Chicanos in other parts of the country that he raise his level of consciousness also reacted. Thus we have writings by Chicano authors stressing the need for those who have had no definite commitment to become involved, even though the issues do not directly affect them. Failing to do so is a kind of refuge by default.[18]

The seeking of refuge after 1848 was a constant preoccupation for Tejanos (Texas Mexicans), especially throughout the nineteenth century. Nepomuceno Cortina's raid on Brownsville in 1859 and his subsequent defeat by the U.S. Army had set a pattern for other Texas-Mexicans who were forced into violent protest against exploitation and injustice. Inevitably, the weight of American authority was too much for a Texas-Mexican to fight. If he was not killed or captured, the man who "defended his right" had either to seek refuge across the Rio Grande in Mexican territory or go *al norte.*

In the 1880s the land to the north again offered economic advantages, and this fact, coupled with the idea of competing on even terms as a cowhand or a railroad worker, presented an alternative that was more appealing than what was available in Texas.

Among the migrants from Mexico during the revolution of 1910 to 1920 were peons fleeing a *hacendado* system, but in Texas they found an even more rigid and cruel ranching system. The peasants who made their way into the Great Plains and the Midwest in some cases found conditions of farm life unlike any previously known to them. At times they worked and ate with—and in many cases shared the homes of—the landowners, and they would never be the same again. Upon returning from their refuge, they would talk of the great opportunity and the hard work that they found in the Great Plains and the Midwest, where, according to them, the dignity of the common man was an accepted fact.

But the refuge had its drawbacks. There was isolation from their own culture. There were subtle prejudices. The Chicanos did not own the land. They were few in number. There was a cultural loss. There was change. Still, Chicano literature is replete with examples demonstrating as historical fact that the Great Plains and the Midwest provided an escape (sometimes an illusion), a terrain, and a host society that tested an individual but offered him or her a better opportunity to compete on equal terms.

For two decades in my own life, the shout every spring of *"Vámonos p'al norte"* opened up visions of adventure, work, money, new people to meet, new situations, new land. It is impossible to imagine Chicano literature without the migrant worker. And it is impossible to imagine the migrant worker without the myriad notions of a refuge in the Great Plains. The idea of refuge is, above all, one more step toward the intellectual emancipation that is basic to the tradition of Chicano literature.

NOTES

1. Ernesto Galarza, "The Roots of Migration," in *Aztlán: An Anthology of Mexican American Literature,* ed. Luis Valdez and Stan Steiner (New York: Alfred A. Knopf, 1972), p. 128.

2. Manuel Gamio, "Narración personal de Elías Garza," in *Literature Chicana; texto y contexto,* ed. Antonia Castañeda Shular, Tomás Ybarra-Frausto, and Joseph Sommers, (Englewood Cliffs, New Jersey: Prentice-Hall, 1972), p. 19.

3. Tomás Ybarra-Frausto, "Cuando vivo el alambre, vino el hambre," in *Literatura Chicana*, p. 208.

4. Rolando Hinojosa-Smith, "E Pluribus Vitae," in *Revista Chicano Riqueña* 1, no. 2 (1973): 14, 15.

5. Rolando Hinojosa-Smith, *Klail City y sus alrededores* (Havana: Casa de los américas, 1976), pp. 88–106.

6. Luis Valdez, "Songs of Exile," in *Aztlán,* p. 131.

7. Joseph Sommers, "El corrido de Kiansis," in *Literatura Chicana,* pp. 210–11.

8. Francisco Rios, "The Mexican in Fact, Fiction and Folklore," in *Voices* (Berkeley, California: Quinto Sol Publications, 1971), pp. 59–73.

9. Antonia Castañeda Shular, "Lo mero principal," in *Literatura Chicana,* pp. 93–94.

10. Américo Paredes, *A Texas-Mexican Cancionero* (Urbana: University of Illinois Press, 1976), pp. 25–26.

11. Tino Villanueva, "De sol a sol," in *Revista Chicano Riqueña* 2, no. 2 (1974): 17–18.

12. Tomás Rivera, *The Earth Did Not Part* (Berkeley, California: Quinto Sol Publications, 1971).

13. Tomás Rivera, "Las salamandras," in *Festival de Foricanto 1* (Los Angeles: Southern California Press, 1976), p. 23.

14. Tomás Rivera, "Odio," in *El grito* 3 (Fall 1969): 60.

15. Javier Aréchiga, "Poetry," in *Revista Chicano Riquêna* 1, no. 2 (1973): 25–28.

16. La Malinche is the name bestowed by the Aztecs on Doña

Marina, a woman given to Cortez before the capture of what is today
Mexico City in 1519–20. She symbolizes the surrender of one culture
to another.

17. Raul Salinas, "A Trip through the Mind Jail," in *Aztlán,* pp.
339–44.

18. Frank Pino, "El teatro," in *Revista Chicano Riquêna* 1, no. 2
(1973): 11–13.

The Contributors

VIRGINIA FAULKNER was a professor of English at the University of Nebraska–Lincoln and editor-in-chief of the University of Nebraska Press. Among her many original writings and editions were *Roundup: A Nebraska Reader* (1957) and *Willa Cather's Collected Short Fiction, 1892–1912* (1970).

CHESTER J. FONTENOT, JR., is an associate professor of English and coordinator of the Afro-American Literature Program at the University of Illinois at Urbana-Champaign. He is the author of *Frantz Fanon: Language as the God Gone Astray in the Flesh* (1979).

FREDERICK C. LUEBKE is a professor of history at the University of Nebraska–Lincoln and acting director of the Center for Great Plains Studies. His books include *Bonds of Loyalty: German Americans and World War I* (1974).

BARBARA HOWARD MELDRUM is a professor of English at the University of Idaho. Her essays have been published in the *Prairie Schooner, Heritage of Kansas,* and other journals.

JOHN R. MILTON is a professor of English at the University of South Dakota. Among his books are *South Dakota: A Bicentennial History* (1977) and *The Novel of the American West* (1980).

PAUL A. OLSON is Foundation Professor of English at the University of Nebraska–Lincoln. A specialist in medieval literature, he has also published extensively in education and American Indian studies.

PAUL REIGSTAD is a professor of English at Pacific Lutheran University. He is the author of *Rølvaag: His Life and Art* (1972).

TOMÁS RIVERA is chancellor of the University of California–Riverside. A widely published poet, novelist, and scholar, Dr. Rivera is a distinguished student of Chicano experience in the United States.

DOROTHY BURTON SKÅRDAL teaches at the American Institute of the University of Oslo, Norway. She is the author of *The Divided Heart: Scandinavian Immigrant Experience through Literary Sources* (1974).

BERNICE SLOTE is professor emeritus of English at the University of Nebraska–Lincoln. Editor of the *Prairie Schooner* from 1963 to 1980, she is the author of *Keats and the Dramatic Principle* (1958) and editor of several books on Willa Cather.

Index

143